# The World of the Aging

## Information Needs and Choices

CELIA HALES-MABRY

American Library Association
Chicago and London 1993

The paper used in this publication meets the minimum requirements of American National Standard for Information Sciences—Permanence of Paper for Printed Library Materials, ANSI Z39.48-1984. ∞

Cover designed by Richmond Jones

Composed by Publishing Services, Inc., Bettendorf, Iowa
in Goudy Oldstyle and Leawood
on Xyvision/Linotype L330

Printed on 50-pound Finch Opaque, a pH-neutral stock,
and bound in 10-point C1S cover stock
by IPC, St. Joseph, Michigan

**Library of Congress Cataloging-in-Publication Data**

Hales-Mabry, Celia.
The world of the aging : information needs and choices / by Celia Hales-Mabry.
p. cm.
Includes index.
ISBN 0-8389-0623-0 (alk. paper)
1. Aged—United States—Information services. 2. Libraries and the aged—United States. I. Title.
HQ1064.U5H192 1993
305.26'0973—dc20 93-9100



Printed in the United States of America.

97 96 95 94 93 5 4 3 2 1

To the older adults in my life:
Joyce Hales, and Paul and Elizabeth Mabry;
and the one so recently watching from the other side,
Ed Hales

And to my husband, Paul:
"Grow old along with me!
The best is yet to be. . . ."
(Browning)

# CONTENTS

# PREFACE

This book is intended, first of all, for librarians, for whom information is our main business. But I hope it will also find a welcome audience among administrators, educators, and service providers in the field of gerontology. These latter individuals need to spend quite a bit of time understanding the interactive informational patterns of their clientele, and this book provides insight into these patterns of behavior through a culling of the literature and a shaping of the material not found heretofore. The central thesis of the book can be stated as follows: Although information is fundamental to our society, few have noted that its lack is the basis for most perceived problems. Given sufficient information, most of the troublesome issues with which we (and older adults) contend on a daily basis would, if not dissipate, at least become more manageable. The more information that is brought to bear on a problem, the more likely a solution will be found. This controlling idea explains in great measure the optimistic tenor of my words throughout the text.

My editor at the American Library Association, Herbert Bloom, has pointed out that there is a "librarian's assumption" operating in this thesis. He notes that the gathering of additional information pursuant to the solving of problems can be threatening because it is possible that such information will be destabilizing, especially to older adults. Librarians such as I, however, operate under the tenet that information is good, and we are inclined to offer as much as a library user will accept. This notion carries over into this book, of course.

This book is two steps removed from the original research; I have relied strongly upon analyses of the primary research and reviews of the literature provided in monographs written by social science academicians. The writing is heavily footnoted because I sought consistently and carefully to ensure that the intellectual thought of others was clearly acknowledged. If I erred at any point, I sincerely regret the lapse in attribution.

I planned this book some five years before I actually started writing it; my then-boyfriend and now-husband Paul assisted me in developing the concept. It was not until the University of Minnesota granted me a three-month professional development leave in the summer of 1990 that I had the uninterrupted time to begin a major writing project. The final writing has taken more than two additional years.

I am a librarian by profession, and I practice that profession currently. My educational background is in library science (and, before that, English and American literature), with heavy research interest in information services for older adults. The research interest began more than a decade ago for my dissertation in library science at Florida State University (with Dr. Ron Blazek as advisor) and has continued in the years since.

I wish to thank my colleagues in Wilson Library Reference Services at the University of Minnesota for providing the very congenial atmosphere in which I have worked on this book, and for filling in on the reference desk in the summer of 1990. They are: Karen Beavers, Mary Combs, Susan Gangl, Susan Hoffman, Bruce Kahn, Kay Kane, Barbara Kautz, Loralee Kerr, Mary Koenig-Loring, Eugene Leadon, Dianne Legg, Dennis Lien, Mary Lee McLaughlin, Janet Roseen, Julia Schult, Lynn Skupeko, Charles Spetland, Alice Wilcox, and Mary Pat Winters. It is a continuing pleasure to work with these individuals.

Jean Cornn and Allan Kleiman, former chairs of the American Library Association's Reference and Adult Services (RASD) Library Services to an Aging Population Committee, provided feedback on the section within devoted to library service to the aging. Jean is a branch manager with the Atlanta Public Library, and Allan is Chief, Services to the Aging, Brooklyn Public Library.

My wonderful husband, Paul Mabry, has been with me every step of the way. He listened attentively innumerable times as I thought aloud about a current dilemma in my writing, and he then added his insight as a psychologist to mine as a librarian. For his assistance and emotional support, and always for his love, I am deeply grateful.

# PART I

# INTRODUCTION

Older adults today are receiving unprecedented attention in our society, in part because their clout has increased along with their numbers. Entitlement programs for this group are largely untouched, due to the lobbying efforts of the major associations that speak for the aging. Some may argue that we have gone too far toward assuring a good life-style for those in their twilight years, but others will quickly point to the fact that this "new age" for elders is a very recent phenomenon; historically, the older adult has been among the most impoverished in our society.

It was always an unhappy myth that the elderly were abandoned by their children; now we know that most live within driving distance of at least one child, that most talk to a child by telephone at least weekly, and that many see at least one child weekly.

Enter information, one of our most important, but usually overlooked, commodities. When someone grows older, he or she is faced with unique problems that cry out for solutions. The more information one can obtain about a given difficulty, the more likely a solution can be found. Often the elder solves his or her own problems, but there are times that family members, friends, professionals, and institutions may come to the rescue.

In the first half of this book, we will look at the distinctive features of the elderly as a group—features that influence the receipt of information physiologically, psychologically, and sociologically. What is unique about the way elders seek and receive information? What can we learn from this that will ensure that information will be available in the best form at the time needed? If we as service providers understand the distinctive features of the normal aging process, we will be better able to meet informational needs. And yet we do not have to be information professionals to meet these needs—family and friends can also help meet these needs by understanding the normal processes of aging that affect informational transfer to their elder companions.

In the second half of the book, we will examine the roles of information and the aging in society. First, how is information itself transferred? In what "packages" does it arrive? These packages are discussed extensively in the chapter on mass media. We will then take a close look at the means by which information is transferred by family, friends, and close professional ties. This direct "appeal" for help—or, more precisely, the simple request for information on a one-to-one basis—is at the heart of informal informational sharing. We will examine those institutions in society (churches, synagogues, schools, libraries, and governmental bodies) that seek to respond to the needs of older adults. We will focus on the informational aspects of their service to the aging.

We will then discuss two specific elderly groups that have special informational needs: those persons with severe health problems and those who are minorities in society. Then we will conclude, briefly, by asking, "What does it all mean to information receipt for the aging?"

# CHAPTER 1

# Who Are the Older Adults Who Need Information?

Before we can understand the informational needs of the elderly, we need to ask, Just who are the elderly in our society? What are their characteristics?

## Characteristics of the Older Adult

Donald G. Fowles cites a number of statistics in his *Profile of Older Americans 1991* that are useful to our analysis.[1] The first statistic sets the tone for a growing aging population: Older adults—those sixty-five and over—totalled 31.2 million in 1990, or 12.6 percent of the population of the United States. That's a 22 percent increase of older adults since 1980, as compared to an 8 percent increase of those under sixty-five. As the numbers grow, as we have noted, so too does the clout of the elder in society. By joining associations such as the American Association of Retired Persons, and lobbying for better benefits, the current group of elders have seen their segment of the population move to a more envied position than ever before in history.

There are other reasons for optimism for elders. People are living longer, and are in much better health than ever before. While in 1990 the age segment of sixty-five to seventy-four years old was eight times larger than it was at the turn of the century, the group age seventy-five to eighty-four was thirteen times larger, and the group eighty-five years and older was a phenomenal twenty-four times larger. Fewer than one-third of older persons in 1989 assessed their health as only fair or poor. While many older persons have chronic conditions, these need not be debilitating. Fully eleven of the twelve months are, according to their estimates, spent free of health problems that would limit their life-style.

Because only 12 percent of elders are in the labor force—and half of those are part-time employees—much time can be spent in their own pursuits.

The majority of individuals live in families, although about one-third (most of whom are women) live alone. The specter of the nursing home does not have to be as fearful for the average elder as, unfortunately, it frequently is: only 5 percent of individuals aged sixty-five and older live in institutions. (This percentage, as we could guess, increases with age.)

Almost 90 percent of elders are white; about 8 percent are African-American, and the remaining 3 percent are of other races. Hispanic people (who can be of any race) represent 4 percent of the total.

Where do elders live? About half live in just nine states: California, Florida, New York, Pennsylvania, Texas, Illinois, Ohio, Michigan, and New Jersey. But contrary to the general consensus, most do not move to Sunbelt states for retirement. The elderly, in fact, are less likely to move than other age groups. And when they do, they are likely to move within the same state, or even to another home in the same city. The median net worth of an elderly person (largely tied to the value of his or her home) is $73,500. This compares to $35,800 for the U.S. average.

## Where Do We Go from Here?

With such optimistic statistics, why have the aging been so negatively stereotyped? It takes a while for the general view of a given people to "catch up" with the reality—especially when that reality has changed as rapidly as it has for today's elder. Improvements in health treatment are a major factor in improving the quality of life for the elder. Also important, of course, is a raised standard of living. The extent to which one is free of financial worries is a major predicting factor for satisfaction in life.

## Why Is Informational Transfer Important?

As we have noted, individuals do change as they grow older, and unique problems must be confronted—problems for which the past has failed to provide adequate solutions. With retirement comes a contracting of horizons for both the worker and his or her spouse—there are fewer people to see on a daily basis, and therefore less chance of finding out exactly how to handle a new problem that may arise.

If society remains open to its elders, ready to satisfy their needs as daily they may change, then we can hope that information *will* offer a chance to confront life's challenges that much more effectively. If society shuts the elder down and out, he or she will be lost in a maze of bewilderingly changing circumstances, both within and without. It is up to us to see that this does not happen.

## Note

1. Donald G. Fowles, *A Profile of Older Americans 1991* (Washington, D.C.: Program Resources Department, American Association of Retired Persons and U.S. Department of Health and Human Services, Administration on Aging, [1991]).

# PART II

# THE INFLUENCE OF AGING PROCESSES ON THE RECEIPT OF INFORMATION

In order to lay the groundwork for an understanding of the information-seeking patterns of the older adult in society, we need to examine, first of all, what makes this age group distinctive in regard to informational transfer.

To do that, we will systematically look at the older adult physiologically, psychologically, and sociologically—being careful all the while to couch this analysis in terms of their information-seeking patterns of behavior. There *are* distinguishing features that are both positive and negative, and the more these features are understood, the more likely individuals who are working with the aging will understand problems and concerns of the older generation. We will also note that the features we are describing are for *normal* aging—not illness or pathology; when normal patterns of aging are described, there are indeed many grounds for optimism, and this will become apparent in our discussion. Let us turn, first of all, to physiological influences on informational receipt.

CHAPTER

# 2

# Physiological Influences

A variety of physiological changes accompany the normal aging process. For analyzing factors influencing receipt of information, three fundamental physiological systems must be addressed: vision, audition (hearing), and movement (motor processes). We will first examine the principal changes in these systems that occur in normal aging; we will then note how these changes might be addressed by the elderly themselves and by the family, friends, and professionals who assist them. While health problems affect many older adults, we will not focus on disease per se because the effects are so diverse as to render a summary discussion worthless; no illness is universal with the aging. (A general discussion of the informational problems affecting disabled elderly, who belong mostly to the oldest individuals, can be found in chapter 9.) Only changes that occur naturally through the aging process itself, and that affect all older adults more or less indiscriminately, will be our concern in this chapter.

## Vision

Visual problems demand particularly difficult adjustments for older people of every age, especially if reading has been important in their earlier years. But any individual who grows older and has increased trouble seeing is at a great disadvantage in our highly visual world. Getting about—particularly driving an automobile—can be threatened. And if one has depended upon a spouse to drive, and that individual becomes no longer able, then, of course, two people are affected by a single statistic. (Adequate transportation has been cited in many studies as one of the greatest needs of the elderly.) Poor vision then results in other life changes that can be difficult for the elder, changes that range from increased dependence upon others to a sense of helplessness in the face of everyday tasks, such as reading the newspaper or reading directions for taking medication. Certainly vision is fundamental to gathering information.

What changes occur normally in the aging eye? The loss of visual acuity is the most obvious. This is the type of vision that is tested on the familiar Snellen wall chart, the one with the big "E" on top. Acuity declines slightly from early adulthood to the fifties, and then drops off more rapidly after age sixty. There is good news, too, however. According to the famous Duke longitudinal study, only among the very old was somewhat impaired, uncorrectable acuity the rule. More than three-fourths of the subjects in their sixties and more than half in their seventies had good corrected vision (20/25 or better) in at least one eye. By contrast, in the group over eighty, only slightly more than one-third did.[1]

The inability to see near objects clearly, *presbyopia,* is common in the aging process, with the first signs of this condition appearing in the early forties. This normal aging trait is generally easily corrected with glasses. For the older adult who has reached age sixty, however, other vision problems develop that cannot be so easily corrected. These include the inability to see clearly in dim light, the inability to distinguish colors (particularly blue and green), sensitivity to glare, and problems with "accommodation," which is the inability to shift vision between objects at varying distances from the viewer. Finally, the field of vision is likely to be narrower for the older adult; one may not be able to see objects on the edge of one's vision.[2]

It is relatively easy to list the types of visual problems that occur; it is less easy to determine exactly which structure has caused the problem, as visual problems are usually based on the integrative working of the various structures of the eye. But let us proceed as far as we can to examine structural changes in the normally aging eye, and the effects of these changes on vision.

### *Overview of the Eye*

The following features are primary to vision and, incidentally, are probably also well known to the layperson, who is likely to recall studying the structures in elementary school, if not later.

### Cornea

The cornea is the clear surface of the eye through which light enters; it is surrounded by the familiar white of the eye, called the *sclera*. The main function of the cornea is to bend, or refract, light toward a focus on the retina. (It does get assistance from the lens, discussed below.) With advancing age the cornea flattens somewhat, causing problems in refraction of the light. There is also a tendency toward astigmatism (or increased astigmatism if the person already has the condition), which means that the curvature of the eye becomes more irregular.

### Iris

The iris is the colored portion of the eye, the part that makes one's eyes brown, blue, or green. The iris is composed of muscle, which features in the action of one of its parts, the pupil. With age there may be a cosmetic change of less brilliancy in the color of the iris. Also occurring is a grayish-yellow ring between the iris and the pupil that may reduce peripheral vision.

### Pupil

The pupil contracts and expands to optimize sight under varying light conditions. By so doing, it regulates the amount of light reaching the retina. The pupil reduces in size with age, a characterisitc that limits vision by reducing the amount of light entering the eye. With an attendant coloring of the lens (see below), it has been found that a sixty-year-old person's retina receives only 30 percent as much light as that of a twenty-year-old.[3] The greatest impact is when the aged person wants to see in dim light and may find this difficult or even impossible.

### Lens

The lens is composed of clear protein. It provides fine adjustment of focus for different viewing distances. The yellowing of the lens causes the so-called yellow filter effect, which alters color perception. Older persons can therefore often distinguish reds and yellows much better than blues, greens, or purple. Glare also may be a problem because as the lens becomes more opaque, the rays of light hitting it are scattered. Another accelerating change involving the lens is increasing farsightedness (presbyopia, mentioned above). Apparent even in one's early forties, this effect can be compounded by problems with accommodation, the ability to shift from far to near vision and vice versa. Problems with accommodation are caused by increased rigidity of the lens. Rather than bulging or flattening as in the young eye, the older adult's eye will become less able to "bulge out," which would allow focus on near objects.

### Vitreous Body

The vitreous body, comprising most of the volume of the eye, lies between the lens and the retina. It is relatively transparent. Most of the shape of the eye is attributable to this structure. As one ages, the vitreous body becomes less transparent, causing a scattering of light rays that leads to blurring of vision. "Floaters," tiny bits of matter that cross the field of vision and that are not uncommon at any age, may increase in number and become irritating, although not dangerous.

### Retina

The retina is photosensitive tissue at the back of the eye and is composed of several parts, including the familiar rods and cones that determine sensitivity to light illumination as well as color perception. Vision in dim light is due to the rods, while the cones function mainly in bright light. Of particular concern is the loss of rods and cones. Adaptation to both light and darkness becomes particularly problematic; aged people do not see in dim light as well as the young do, regardless of how long the adjustment period, and emerging into the light from a dark theater, for example, can be particularly painful due to glare. In addition, blood vessels and capillaries in the retina narrow and some atrophy occurs.

## *Practical Implications*

Many of the visual changes in older adulthood may be accounted for by changes in just two structures: the pupil and the lens.[4] The pupil becomes reduced in size, letting in dramatically less light; and the lens becomes thicker, more opaque, and more yellowish in color, further reducing the light and the clarity of the image that focuses on the retina. One obvious compensation would be to increase the lighting in the environment used by older adults. However, this will not always work because more lighting is likely to increase glare—a problem, as we have seen, for aging eyes. So the amount and type of illumination in a given setting will need careful monitoring. Differences in contrast are important for the older adult. Low contrast may, in fact, require twice as much light as the more normal medium and high contrast. One common example of this is the fact that letters on a page need to be strongly black; gray letters, showing low contrast with the white page, will be difficult to read.

To reduce glare as much as possible, lighting should be more yellowish than blue, since bluish light is scattered more (the factor that causes glaring) by the lens of the older person. The drawback, however, is that yellowish light, compounded with the elder's yellowish lens, makes yellow colors appear more yellow, and greens, blues, and violets more difficult to discriminate. Accurate color perception thus is a major problem for the elderly, and may be made more difficult by trying to manipulate the environment. Thus, what improves one type of visual problem may actually exacerbate another.

Depth perception is sometimes affected by the aging process, making cues from the environment problematic and contributing to difficulties in driving an automobile. Because the elder's smaller pupil lets in less light than a younger person's, an elder is at a greater disadvantage when driving, all other things being equal. Road signs, for example, cannot be seen well at night or at dusk, in rain or snow, but there may also be a problem in bright sunlight, when glare is likely. Adaptation to changes in lighting is also affected, making entry into and emergence from a tunnel, for example, hazardous. Poor peripheral vision means that information from the sides of one's visual field may go unnoticed. And loss of the eye's ability to accommodate may result in problems when, for example, the elder driver glances at the dashboard after looking at the road. Although all of these factors would point toward greater accidents for elders, it is reassuring to know that such is not always the case, particularly with the young-old.[5] The reasons are unclear but perhaps lie in many elderly drivers' greater experience, greater caution, or refusal to drive in adverse conditions.

A number of relatively simple things can be done by the family member or professional in presenting visual information to the elderly person. First in importance is good lighting in the environment, but not too much so that glare becomes a problem. In presenting information, one should keep within the visual field, neither too far to the right or left, and particularly not too high (perception of objects at the top of the visual field is reduced considerably). Keep information relatively uncluttered, allowing the individual to focus on the few items of importance.[6] If color is desired, use bright colors, preferably yellows and reds, and avoid blues, greens, and violets, especially those in muted hues. Dark objects on light ones, or light on dark, will offer good contrast, and thus be more readily seen. Large print for calendars, clocks, books, telephone dials, etc., is readily available and should be used more often than is actually the case. There are a wide number of visual aids such as magnifiers to assist the moderately visually impaired. And regular changes of prescription in eyewear—reflecting, of course, the changing visual perception of the elder—is highly recommended.[7]

The main problem in helping the elderly person with visual problems is not that we do not know how to present information in an easily understood form but rather that we do not even consider doing so—a problem of insensitivity that borders on unforgivable. For example, government forms intended for the elderly are all too often printed in small letters and with poor contrast (gray letters rather than strong black). The lettering on prescription-drug containers is, again, small and therefore frequently unreadable. It will take greater advocacy for the older adult, and perhaps their own further empowerment, to effect solutions to these common, daily nuisances of life. Advocacy for and empowerment of the elderly are both growing rapidly, and so we have reason to predict that changes for the better will be forthcoming.

## Hearing

When asked which is the most important sensory ability, the layperson is likely to name vision. However, research has determined that hearing is most important in one's interaction with his or her environment, especially in very important everyday communication with other people. Any impairment is likely to have a devastating effect on the older adult.

More than half of all older adults suffer from some degree of hearing loss. This is immediately noticeable in public from the large number of aging individuals who wear hearing aids; people over sixty-five are thirteen times more likely to wear a hearing aid than younger people.[8] Yet most elderly do not have truly debilitating hearing loss. As in visual problems, it is the very old who are most afflicted; according to one highly reliable study, 25 percent have profound hearing loss, as opposed to 12 percent of the young-old.[9] It should be pointed out, however, that research studies have differed widely over the amount and degree of hearing loss reported among the aging; some studies show a high of 33 percent of over-sixty-five adults may have hearing loss that causes "unfavourable social consequences."[10] Studies, however, with this high figure include self-reporting, normally a less-reliable basis. Overall, we may conclude that between one-tenth and one-third of older people have some degree of hearing loss that affects their daily life—a substantial number, but not a majority.

The common cause of normal hearing loss is excess noise throughout one's lifetime. Environmental differences have led to a differential in hearing loss between men and women. Older men have been exposed, on the average, to higher levels of noise in their work environment, creating greater hearing loss than for women.

The most common type of hearing loss is universal in aging, and is called *presbycusis*. It is the inability to hear high-pitched sounds as well as low; thus female voices can be more difficult to hear than male. There may be an accompanying inability to filter out extraneous sounds from the environment. Some individuals who have presbycusis will also experience a sudden abnormal increase in the perception of loudness. This may have social repercussions, as when one who is trying to be heard will suddenly be told to "stop shouting," even though their previous level of sound has not been understood. Presbycusis normally results from deterioration in the inner ear. In some persons, however, there may be hearing loss called "conductive," which results from problems in the middle or outer ear. Let us study the main structures of the ear, with a view toward determining what communication problems may result from dysfunction.

## *Overview of the Ear*

### Outer Ear

The outer ear is composed of that part which can be easily seen from the outside; it is otherwise called the *pinna*. Changes with aging in this part are usually cosmetic and may have only minor repercussions for the individual's hearing. Connecting the outer ear to the middle ear is the auditory canal, which contains the familiar earwax. An increased brittleness in the wax brought on by aging may result in blockage, easily corrected but perhaps the cause of as many as one-third of the cases of hearing loss among the elderly.

### Middle Ear

The mechanical transmission of sound occurs in this part of the ear, which is largely an air-filled cavity, except for the three small bones comprising the *ossicle*. The ossicle amplifies the sound and transmits it from the eardrum to the membrane , or "open window," that separates the middle ear from the inner ear. There are normal changes related to age, and as these occur, there is less-efficient transmission of sound vibrations.

### Inner Ear

The inner ear contains two important structures: the *cochlea*, the part containing the hair cells, which are the auditory receptors; and the semicircular canals, called the *vestibular apparatus*, which determine balance and equilibrium. The hair cells, which actually determine hearing, respond to high, medium, or low tones based on their placement within the cochlea. Thus it is possible to have hearing loss affecting different types of sound. For hearing to occur, nerve impulses must be sent from the auditory nerve to the auditory center of the brain. Presbycusis, which as we have noted is the greatest reason for hearing loss in the aged, results from a loss of hair cells in the cochlea. Those cells responding to high tones go first, followed by the cells responding to medium and low tones.

## *Practical Implications*

Aside from its importance in communicating with people, hearing is an essential means of receiving signals from the world of an orienting or warning nature. Information of this type can often be taken for granted until hearing impairment occurs.

Hearing also improves the quality of one's life, as one listens to music, goes to the theater, watches (and listens to) television, etc. Most important of all, social communication is disrupted if one does not hear well. At this point many forces interplay, including the fact that aging individuals do not, for social reasons, always want to admit that they have not understood something that has been said. The people with whom the older adult is conversing may also not respond well, particularly when the one with hearing loss is only able to understand some of what is said. Such problems are due to perceptual differences in hearing certain letters, as well as variations in background noise.

Many hearing-impaired individuals begin to read lips and watch facial expressions, compensating well before needing something more. Certainly appropriate professional consultation is indicated. Hearing aids amplify sound, which is helpful, although since all sound is amplified, background noise can become distracting.

There are a number of helpful adaptations that a person talking with a hearing-impaired older adult can make. Be patient, repeating as needed, and speak slowly and clearly more than loudly (which can be embarrassing in public). Keep background noise to a minimum, if possible. Try to be sure that the person has understood what has been said, because given our society's fast pace and general disinclination to adapt to handicaps, he or she may be reluctant to ask you to repeat your words. Misunderstanding, in addition to the hearing problem itself, then becomes a barrier. Use gestures as appropriate, for these can be important cues as to what is meant.[11]

## Reaction and Movement

One of the most-studied components of aging is the degree to which one "slows down" in old age. It is, in fact, one of the least-disputed conclusions about the aging process, and now it appears that the only dispute is how best to label the process.[12] As it turns out, studies have shown that it is not the actual physical movement that is most problematic for the elder, but rather it is the impairment that has occurred in the central nervous system that impedes the motor movement. One moves more slowly, therefore, because one is unable to respond to the stimulus as quickly as when younger.

The physiological reasons are speculative but include the following: decline in the nervous system, when neurons and nerve cells die; increase in reflex time for the skeletal muscles; a loss in efficiency in the brain mechanisms that monitor signals from the environment; and a general deterioration of the sensory and motor systems.[13] Nevertheless, these sensory and motor impairments do not have to be a detriment to learning; more often they are problematic when *other people* are brought into play. The individual who is aging has learned how, gradually, to pace his or her life to ongoing sensory and motor limitations; because the change is gradual, accommodation comes easily to most.

Learning is usually affected only by declining eyesight, which can, of course, be a real detriment. The problem is usually the impatience of others. Younger people must slow down their own movements to assist the elder whom they are accompanying, and many find this difficult to do.

Being quick has great behavioral implications for our society; it has been speculated that this one fact of slowness is a major consideration in the age discrimination with which elders must contend. A slower pace puts one "out of sync" with the rest of society, creating impatience among one's faster-moving family and friends.[14]

Simple tasks can be executed more readily than more complex ones, a phenomenon that grows more evident among the aged. Tasks involving a sequence of steps are the most difficult. Experience with a given task, however, can offset this finding and thus allow the elder to compensate in the activities he or she does most often. This slowness is evident in virtually all activities, not just those requiring physical action. There is, however, great variability among the elderly with regard to the degree of slowness. Exercise has been shown to improve response time, enough so that active elderly can perform as well as inactive young people on some tasks.[15]

Another factor influencing the outcome is general health, with those who are fittest doing the best, as would be expected. Practice as well as experience, as we have mentioned, can compensate greatly. Finally, motivation must not be overlooked. Highly motivated older adults are an inspiration to all, peers as well as lazier young companions. These older adults, in effect, make their world "work" despite their limitations.

### *Practical Implications*

Slow behavior has a great influence upon information-seeking patterns, determining how readily the individual will seek to satisfy his or her own needs, and how often those needs will either go unmet or be satisfied by others. A person who takes a long time to walk to the library may decide not to go after all, unless a whole afternoon can be set aside for this activity. Reading speed will be reduced, whether it is the latest novel or a weekly news magazine. Less information will reach the older adult because he or she has only as many hours as anyone else. The older adult who has slowed considerably does, in fact, occupy a different world from others who are younger. And all too often annoyance is the response of those who do not understand or sympathize with this completely normal aging change, one that will come to all who grow older.

The best advice for those interacting with older persons is simply to be patient and accommodating to them, but not patronizing. In many cases, an older individual may not recognize the degree to which he or she has slowed. Occurring gradually and increasing as time goes by, this condition demands that the older adult adjust reactions and movements to the level at which he or she feels most comfortable. This may or may not cause discomfort in those around him, but this accommodation certainly will reduce accidents, particularly falls—a common problem for the elderly. Thus slowness becomes a way of life, but a way of life that allows for gradual adaptation to the aging body in which one is living.

## Summary

We can see that vision, hearing, and movement (and reaction) are all affected by the passage of time, even though the individual may remain disease-free. Normal changes are usually very gradual, allowing time for adjustment on the part of the elder and his or her companions, and even de-emphasizing the fact that there has been any change at all. The human being in normal aging is indeed resilient.

Those with whom elders interact can do their part to ease time's effects. Adapting the environment to the elderly can be effected in rather simple and inexpensive ways, ways that are all too often not even considered by a sometimes insensitive world. And younger people can be more accommodating to the elderly, recognizing, if they are wise, that regardless of our stress-prone and fast-paced world, the older adult who has slowed and may have visual and auditory problems is deserving of our understanding and assistance.

## Notes

1. B. Anderson and Erdman B. Palmore, "Longitudinal Evaluation of Ocular Function," in *Normal Aging II*, ed. Erdman B. Palmore (Durham, N.C.: Duke University Press, 1974).
2. Janet Belsky, *The Psychology of Aging: Theory, Research, and Practice* (Monterey, Calif.: Brooks/Cole, 1984), 72.
3. Sue V. Saxon and Mary Jean Etten, *Physical Change and Aging; A Guide for the Helping Professions*, 2d ed. (New York: Tiresias, 1987), 74.
4. Susan Whitbourne, *The Aging Body: Physiological Changes and Psychological Consequences* (New York: Springer-Verlag, 1985), 166.
5. Ibid., 167, reporting Paul E. Panek et al., "A Review of Age Changes in Perceptual Information Ability with Regard to Driving," *Experimental Aging Research* 3 (November 1977): 387–449.
6. Gloria Sorensen, "Sensory Deprivation," in *Older Persons and Service Providers: An Instructor's Training Guide*, ed. Gloria Sorensen (New York: Human Sciences Press, 1981), 50.
7. Colette Browne and Roberta Onzuka-Anderson, *Our Aging Parents: A Practical Guide to Eldercare* (Honolulu: University of Hawaii Press, 1985), 54.
8. Belsky, *Psychology of Aging*, 78.
9. Ibid.

10. Whitbourne, *Aging Body*, 184, reporting L. Fisch, "Special Senses: The Aging Auditory System," in *Textbook of Geriatric Medicine and Gerontology*, ed. J. C. Brocklehurst (New York: Churchill Livingstone, 1978), 283.
11. Browne and Onzuka-Anderson, *Our Aging Parents*, 57.
12. Waneen W. Spirfuso and Priscilla Gilliam MacRae, "Motor Performance and Aging," in *Handbook of the Psychology of Aging*, 3d ed., ed. James E. Birren and K. Warner Schaie (San Diego: Academic Press, 1990), 192.
13. Barry D. McPherson, *Aging as a Social Process: An Introduction to Individual and Population Aging* (Toronto: Butterworths, 1983), 178.
14. Belsky, *Psychology of Aging*, 85.
15. Jack Botwinick and Martha Storandt, "Cardiovascular Status, Depressive Affect and Other Factors in Reaction," *Journal of Gerontology* 29 (September 1974): 543–48.

CHAPTER

# 3

# Psychological Influences

We will look at psychological influences on the aging process by analyzing two of the primary processes that influence the elder: cognition and personality. In cognition, we find that the outlook is reassuring for most elders, unless pathology intervenes. In personality, we will find that a stable core very similar to the younger self normally accompanies the elder in the culminating years of the life cycle.

## Cognitive Processes

The term *cognitive processes* refers to a group of abilities with their locus in the mind: intelligence, memory, learning, creativity, etc. Part of the difficulty in accurately assessing one's level of functional cognition in late life is due to the imprecision of the instruments used. The tests that are given, whether to determine IQ, memory, or the like, are nearly always designed for a younger age group. Whether or not the tests are fair to elders or even valid to use are major questions. However questionnable the tests might be, though, they are all we have at present. And it is possible, within certain constraints, to use them to make some scientifically based conclusions. These conclusions will assist the older adult and the family, friends, and professionals who are a part of his or her world to place emphasis upon the elder's continuing cognitive strengths and to compensate for any losses due to age. They will also help elders to make more realistic assessments of their cognitive abilities, assessments that lead to far more optimistic conclusions than those found in traditional lay knowledge.

### A Look at the Intellect in Later Life

Whether or not cognitive abilities decline with age is a question fraught with emotional overtones to an extent far greater than the question of physiological change. When one is assessing intelligence, people can get defensive quite readily. This is compounded by the fact that it is no easy matter to access accurately the degree of intellectual functioning in individuals of various ages and ethnic backgrounds. Bias in IQ tests is a very real problem, one that has not been adequately addressed, despite years of attempted "improvements." Due to the nature of testing itself, perhaps no truly bias-free instrument will ever be developed, although we must strive in that direction.

We can conclude that standardized tests prepared for the majority and given to all, minorities included, discriminate; this is no less true for the aged as it is for those of varying ethnic and cultural backgrounds. When older adults are given intelligence tests which are specially prepared to test practical items about which they presumably have more intimate knowledge than younger adults, they are found to be superior. Any discussion, therefore, of attempts to measure intelligence in the elderly must be approached tentatively. Our conclusions cannot be definitive, but they do express some of what we know, given admitted imperfections, and can suggest possible ways to address informational outreach to the aging.

Given that very large disclaimer, what do we know about the intellect of those aged sixty-five and above, as measured by tests? In a nutshell, verbal ability is likely to remain stable or to decline only slightly, if at all, until one is quite advanced in years (a member of the "old-old" population); performance ability, however, is likely to exhibit a precipitous decline for all individuals past young adulthood (early twenties in age). This has come to be known as the "classic aging pattern."[1]

What is the difference between verbal and performance ability? Verbal ability is measured by one's performance on tests of general knowledge, comprehension, arithmetic, verbal analogies, memory, and word definitions. In general, the ability to perform well on this part of an IQ test is based, at least in part, on the fact that the elder's daily life includes practice in doing many of these very tasks. On the IQ test used most often for the elderly—the Wechsler Adult Intelligence Scale

(WAIS)—four of the six subtests of the verbal part remain consistent over the life span (until very old age); only two decline, and this is generally a modest amount. The four subtests on the verbal part that do not show much, if any, decline are all measures of stored knowledge.[2]

Another type of intelligence is measured by performance ability, testing for which speed is important (another variable difficult for the aging). This is measured by tasks that are far removed from the everyday life of the typical older person: copying symbols as fast as possible, identifying the missing items from pictures, arranging sets of blocks and pictures to form a pattern or coherent whole, and solving puzzles. On this part of the WAIS, the aging sustain marked losses in each subtest.

When older adults are given the WAIS, they are compared within their own age range as individuals; the test itself, though, has been validated through various studies involving younger people. For IQ testing to assess intelligence in the general population, two types of studies have been conducted: those in which individuals of different ages are grouped together, and then the groups are compared with one another (called cross-sectional studies); and those in which the same individuals are tested at intervals of time, and then comparisons are drawn (longitudinal studies). The former type of study uniformly draws pessimistic conclusions for the effect of the aging process upon intellect; the latter are kinder in results.

To understand this difference, we must first describe intelligence itself, as characterized in the literature. It is the type of intelligence that reflects the content of the culture, called "crystallized intelligence," that continues to remain optimal throughout most of the life cycle. This is the knowledge that is gained through educational and life experiences. A second type of intelligence, one that measures the capacity to devise a solution to a new problem never before encountered, called "fluid intelligence," is dependent upon a brain at it physiological best. Older adults are at a great disadvantage when this type of intelligence is tested. Why? It is apparent after many tests that while older individuals may not decline appreciably from what they once were, they have never functioned intellectually *as measured on tests* as well as the young of today.[3]

What this most definitely does *not* say is that the elder generation is less genetically "bright" than the generations that follow. What it does say is that the only way we have to measure is by testing, and young people are at a great advantage because of greater levels of schooling and more "test savvy," the likelihood of better health and therefore better performance on test-taking, and the like. This accounts for the relatively lower results for the aging on cross-sectional studies. In longitudinal testing, by contrast, only those in the best condition (by and large) continue to survive and to take the tests, creating a more positive result for the aging. (Health is a major influence upon how well one does on tests.) All in all, however, longitudinal tests are superior, and the evidence from them can be taken more seriously, because each individual is used as his or her own control.

In addition to the types of disadvantages indicated above, there are other reasons for the sometimes poor showing of elders in IQ testing. Most of the aging have had far fewer years of formal schooling than younger age groups. Presumably, the tests reflect school content which many elders never received. Moreover, test-taking skill is involved, obviously, and the more years of schooling, the more likely that one will be proficient in this skill. Elders are more likely to approach test-taking cautiously and are therefore less likely to guess at answers, which puts them at a disadvantage on many tests. Anxiety also interferes with test performance, and the elderly will likely have a higher level than young people, in part because testing the intellect is so threatening to them. The aging show fatigue more easily than young people, making for another compounding factor leading to lower test scores. Fatigue may be associated with illness, and the degree of health determines, probably more than any other extraneous factor, the reason for poor showings. Even slight physical impairment has been shown to adversely affect IQ scores.[4] All in all, there are sufficient reasons to show that taking tests is a far more formidable undertaking for the elderly than for their younger counterparts, and this leads to speculation that the results are skewed negatively.

Can anything be done to ensure that such declines occur at a minimum? First, good health promotes a healthy mind, and there is ample evidence that optimal mental functioning occurs when the body is performing well. Second, we can make a comparison to children's performance on IQ tests that is instructive: the more varied and rich the environment of the child, the higher his or her ability as measured on IQ tests. It would seem likely that the more intellectually stimulating and complex the environment of the elder—the more he or she "exercises" the mind—the less decline in intellectual prowess. This is folk knowledge that is backed up by solid research.

While the above discussion suggests various ways in which the aging are at a disadvantage in IQ testing, this is not necessarily cause for concern. The best news is that those parts of the test that measure abilities that are used in everyday life by the elderly show little or no decline—welcome news for information assimilation. It is likely that physiological changes in the brain and nervous system put the elderly at a disadvantage in novel situations, but this is a decline that occurs over the whole range of adult life, from the early twenties onward, and certainly no one questions that the prime of most individuals occurs much later than the twenties. Ultimately, therefore, we can conclude that there is little cause for alarm in regard to problem-solving abilities in older adulthood; individuals can and do use their hard-won experience to function at their best in a changing environment.

### *Practical Implications of Intelligence Research*

What does this say for the elder who is processing information in daily life? Basically, it means that one does *not* have to be fearful that one's intellectual powers are in decline. The types of cognition called upon in daily life are rarely on the decline, while performance abilities have been declining since one's early twenties (a somewhat reassuring fact, in light of the realization that one's most productive years are well beyond that tender age). Part of the "skill" of retaining intellectual mastery in later life is related to the efficiency with which information has always been processed by a given individual.

### *Learning and Memory*

One researcher has likened the relationship between learning and memory to a "chicken and egg" situation. In this description, learning is equated with the acquisition of information or behavior, while memory involves the storage and retention of the learned behavior.[5] In order for any specified information to be learned, it must be stored in memory; and in order to demonstrate that the information has indeed been learned, it must be retrieved from memory. This retrieval requires demonstration or performance, and it is at this point that one has difficulty assessing the reasons for learning or memory failure. Has the information never been learned? Or was it learned but not remembered? Or, finally, has the information been learned and stored in memory, but cannot (for whatever reasons) be retrieved? As we shall see, sorting out these variables for assessing the aging adult's learning and memory is not easy.

Laboratory experiments designed to test learning and memory usually are verbal, which means, as will be recalled, that older adults are not immediately at a disadvantage because these are the abilities that they continue to use in daily life. The individual is presented with words, letters, or nonsense syllables either orally or visually; after a number of these have been presented, the individual is asked to recall what he or she has observed. A second common technique is somewhat easier for the subject: he or she is given information and then is asked later only to recognize what has been heard or seen. (There are, of course, numerous variations on these models.) In demonstrating what has been learned, recall may be tested without any assistance or "hints" from the investigator, or cues may be given.

The general slowing of the nervous system that we have earlier observed affects the outcome of the testing of older adults. They may not actually have more trouble learning than a younger person, but they may take longer to commit given bits of information to memory, and longer to retrieve what has been learned. As we shall see, setting down memories (and, therefore, learning) does occur in "stages." If interruption occurs before the new information has been sufficiently "laid down," as it were, the memory will not be encoded sufficiently for the information to be recalled later. As with intelligence testing, if older adults are not timed but rather can set their own pace, they will do much better in displaying that information has indeed been learned.

Aside from this matter of slowing, older adults have some deficit in determining relevant from irrelevant information in a test situation. Distraction can be a problem, and so if this is kept to a minimum, the aged do better. Other variables in the testing situation that determine how well one performs include the level of motivation (which, if high, can lead to overarousal and if low, can mean that individuals will not try very hard), the level of intelligence and of education (the higher, the better), and, finally, the state of health (poor health almost universally means poor test results).[6] Low motivation is particularly troublesome for experimenters, as older people have little patience with learning exercises that have little or no relevance to them.[7] Finally, it should be noted that most studies of memory and learning skill have been cross-sectional—i.e., comparing older adults as a group to groups of younger people at various age ranges—and this, as we have seen in intelligence testing, leads to more pessimistic results for the older adults.

How does memory actually work? How does one store information? The truth is that this mystery has not been solved in a way that takes into account all of the many variables that exist; the brain is an infinitely challenging organ. Yet psychologists have identified a model that allows us to discuss the three stages of memory that can be observed.[8] The first stage involves the immediate storage in the senses, lasting one-third to two seconds only. From here, we proceed to the second stage of memory, in which information is recorded in *primary memory*. Primary memory represents all that can be kept in conscious awareness at a given time. This is the knowledge that one has of his or her immediate environment; it is not a recall of daily events so much as it is the "recall" of the events that are happening *now*. Finally, if learning is to take place, we proceed to the third stage, in which information is committed to *secondary memory*. This involves short- and long-term storage, and is what is generally termed "memory" in everyday understanding.

In addition to these three stages, there appear to be different *types* of memory, especially within the secondary memory. It is commonly recognized that older people recall episodes from the past relatively easily; even when memory of daily events is impaired (for example, by a stroke), the individual is likely to recall details of those life events most important to him or her. This propensity is termed *episodic memory*. The type of memory most affected by impairment is the so-called common knowledge shared by most people in regard to the immediate environment; this type of memory is called *semantic*.

Testing in the laboratory has revealed that recall tests are the most problematic for elders. This means that retrieval of information is deficient. Actually, though, this type of test is the most difficult for all ages, as any college professor can attest. Students who have to respond in essays (thereby exhibiting recall without hints) do more poorly than students who answer multiple-choice questions (where only recognition is required). So the reason for poorer performance may be linked to poor habits of learning rather than to learning deficit, per se. And it has been found that older adults do better on subsequent testing after they have been coached in various tricks of learning, such as making analogies or pairing items to be remembered.[9] This amounts therefore to the need of elders for better encoding in memory; again, as we might guess and have seen repeatedly in testing, educational levels interact to form yet another variable.

There is, therefore, no consensus about the extent and nature of learning and memory deficits in the aging, although some slowing is believed to occur. The common fear of the old, that they are losing their memory for the details of everyday life, is likely to produce an overreaction unless pathology is actually present. While some slippage probably occurs in normal aging, it is not nearly as widespread as is feared by the elderly. Once pathology such as depression is ruled out, the slippage that does occur can be compensated for by some simple techniques of practice and training. In one particularly optimistic study, cognitive skill training actually erased all performance differences between the young and the old.[10] Enriching the environment has a similar effect; as found in intelligence testing, if the older person remains active and energetically engaged, there is less slippage.[11]

Fears about forgetting are widespread among the older community, which is regrettable. If the older adult knows that learning and memory deficits, or forgetting, are not profound in the normal aging process—a conclusion that we have drawn from the research evidence—he or she will not compound any miminal problem by worrying about it.

### Practical Implications of Research in Memory and Learning

If one has developed memory-coping skills (note-taking, "tricks" to aid memory, etc.), the likelihood of remaining vigorous in intellectual matters is reassuring. What does cause alarm is the fear that one's memory is declining. It is perhaps not widely recognized that one cannot think effectively when tense; if one "freezes up" in trying to recall a date, a name, a phone number, the given information is even less likely to be retrieved. How many times has one failed to retrieve a given fact on demand, although the answer is "on the tip of the tongue"? Certainly often, but it is usually only elders who become alarmed at this "evidence" that they are slipping. Younger people just shrug it off (unless there is pathology in the family). We would do well to suggest to elders that disregarding this minor retrieval failure (given such trivial, anxiety-ridden evidence) in fact is appropriate to them as well.

### Creativity

In the section on the intellect, we defined one type of intelligence—fluid intelligence—as a capacity to devise a solution to a new problem never before encountered. This ability would appear to be uniquely necessary to creative endeavor, and since older adults are recognized to have deficits in this area, we might conclude that their range of creativity would be limited. Since we have many examples of older adults who have excelled in creative endeavors in the arts (Grandma

Moses, Arthur Rubinstein, George Burns) as well as the sciences (Margaret Mead, Albert Einstein, B. F. Skinner), obviously what appears probable from the initial evidence is not the whole truth. For some, their best work has come at an advanced age.

There are many other variables that affect one's creativity: motivation, enthusiasm, physical stamina, etc. In some types of creativity, immersion in the content of one's profession is important. Moreover, the length of one's life, or life experiences in and of themselves, can be crucial. While all of these factors can be important, these last two factors, perhaps more than the others, help determine the level of creativity for various professions in different decades of life.

Early flawed research seemed to indicate that creativity peaked at a particularly early age, in young adulthood.[12] This is actually true only for certain subject areas, and may be a by-product of child prodigy cases. For the vast majority of subject areas, creativity is *enhanced* by the experiences of later life. Unfortunately, the earlier research received much media attention, and as a result, the incorrect conclusions of the study have remained part of popular folk wisdom. Later, quite different results were found, using different methods. Rather than in young adulthood, creativity was found to peak for most professions in the middle years—the forties and the fifties, the years that are also the most productive. (Creativity and productivity were found to correlate.)[13] To break down the figures, it was found that the peak for mathematics and chemistry, for example, is in the thirties and forties, while the peak for literature and history (where experience and reflection count a great deal) is as late as the sixties.

Because these investigations have focused exclusively upon those highly creative individuals who have received acclaim, the conclusions that may be drawn for more ordinary people are uncertain. Nevertheless, there is much anecdotal and scientific research to conclude that older adults are not necessarily at a disadvantage in creative endeavors because one type of intelligence (fluid intelligence), as measured on IQ tests, is impaired relative to younger people.

### *Practical Implications of Research in Creativity*

Here is virtually conclusive evidence that tests do not accurately measure creativity in elders. The type of intelligence that presumably would be involved in creativity—fluid intelligence—is where elders are at the greatest disadvantage due to natural aging processes in the brain since young adulthood. Yet, the anecdotal evidence is strong that many aging adults do, in fact, reach great heights of creative endeavor late in life. Perhaps it is conceivable that only in the final years can one draw upon a lifetime of mental prowess in assimilating knowledge to lead, in turn, to those great genius-like breakthroughs. It is believed that genius (highly correlated with creativity) is best exemplified when one has mastered the knowledge and then let one's mind "play" with the facts. Allowing this intuitive factor free rein may be crucial in determining how creative one is or can become. Certainly the aging can draw upon a lifetime of knowledge, then put their own stamp upon that knowledge, to formulate truly creative innovations.

### *Summary*

We have seen, therefore, that in the three major areas of cognitive prowess—the intellect, learning and memory, and creativity—aging people have good reason to be optimistic. The culprit is not normal aging, which can have benign effects, but more general declines in health with accompanying diseases. Decline in intelligence, as measured by IQ tests (which have problems of validity), occurs obviously in one type of intelligence only and is readily compensated for in the everyday world by the elder's greater experience and by one's remaining active and involved. Learning and memory have a similar prognosis based on the same general scientific rule: there will probably be some decline, but nothing substantial without a pathological cause. The evidence for continued contributions through creative endeavor is perhaps the most optimistic of all, in part because we have such striking anecdotal evidence from aging individuals who are involved in creative professions. And the scientific evidence backs up the likelihood of greater creative success at a later period in life than would be predicted through the measures that we use for assessing intelligence, learning, and memory.

## Personality

Let us now investigate the older adult's personality as manifested both internally and externally. The internal changes are the most significant in determining the degree to which adjustment to change will be successful. External changes involve life transitions that are sometimes out of the range of choice, particularly in regard to timing: retirement, death of a spouse, institutionalization.

### *The Older Adult Internally: Continuity and Change*

Does the process of aging cause changes in personality? Are older adults similar or dissimilar to the way they were in young and middle adulthood? The consensus is that personality in healthy adults is amazingly stable over the lifespan, including the latter years.[14] If a person has been well-adjusted at thirty, he or she is likely to be similarly well adjusted at sixty-five. This is not to say that some changes do not occur, however; any individual must adjust to changing conditions, and change is a part of everyone's life, including, perhaps especially, the older adult's. The older person, in fact, has to adjust to more rapid change in society than ever before. And, moreover, there are major predictable life changes that come to most older individuals: retirement, the deaths of a spouse and of friends, colleagues, etc. We might conclude, therefore, that while personality patterns will remain generally consistent if there is no pathology, the older adult will seek to adjust to life change and will thus be changed, albeit in limited ways.

### *A Preliminary Look at Research*

Relatively little research has focused specifically on the older adult's personality, and much of that which does exist can be criticized methodologically. We must frequently extrapolate from small samples of older people. Much research has been cross-sectional, a method that is sometimes less reliable, particularly for elders, than longitudinal methods. And men have been studied more frequently than women. Given all of these constraints, what can we say about personality change?

As indicated above, stability is the norm in the absence of health problems.[15] In fact, there is some indication that individuals (especially highly educated men) may make some attempt to increase consistency in action and thought as they age. This will not always be successful, however, either for groups as a whole or for individuals. An entire older adult group may change in some trait, but the individuals within that group may not change positions relatively. For example, there is some evidence to suggest that older men are less aggressive than they were in their younger years. It is quite conceivable, however, that in a given sample, the same individuals will still, within that group, be "most aggressive," although all adult males in the sample may be relatively less aggressive than they were when younger.

One important study has found that social, adaptive behavior may remain relatively stable, but that inner, psychic change may be rather radical. This study found that older individuals become less interested in the outer world and more preoccupied with themselves.[16] While at first glance this appears to be a negative finding, it can actually be seen to work to the elder's advantage as he or she adjusts to change. (It does bring up an important debate over the disengagement theory, discussed below.) The relationship between the individual's psyche and the outer world has been studied to determine the extent to which they influence one another.

The consensus now for the relationship between the individual's personality and the exterior world is that the personality traits of a given person influence behavior and adaptation to his or her life situation, while the situation itself helps to determine which traits will actually manifest themselves.

An important difference, as suggested above, has been found in individuals according to their sex. Older men have mellowed, in that their aggressive tendencies are reduced in old age; simultaneously and perhaps linked to this change in the male, is the fact that assertiveness on the part of women is generally greater. This may be due to the fact that women of an older generation are no longer nurturing children, but it may also be due to the fact that their own aggressiveness was masked when their husbands were manifesting aggressive tendencies.

### Theories of Personality

The disengagement theory says that older adults, as they age, will undergo an inevitable withdrawal from their society. The equilibrium that existed within a younger person in relation to the larger society will therefore undergo radical alteration as that person ages. In absolute terms, the theory has been disproved; individuals do not always undergo disengagement,[17] but we must then ask to what extent most individuals in fact do disengage. The well-known Duke studies suggest that health is the vital factor, not age per se. It is true that disengagement occurs in increasing measure in the older population, but usually as a function of their relative health.

In reaction to the disengagement theory, the activity theory has been put forward: Older persons who are more active will be more mentally alert than those who are disengaged.[18] Obviously, this is a matter of personality structure. A well-adjusted older person may be quite satisfied to be disengaged, but a poorly adjusted elder might need to be taken out of himself or herself and into activity, in order to sustain optimal life satisfaction. Morale and activity thus are not necessarily synonymous.

### *Types of Personality*

Studies of personality types are highly theoretical, but the history of these studies indicates that later studies are dependent upon the earlier models, at least as a starting point. Let us trace the history of some of the most important models in order to determine what conclusions may be drawn from a theoretical framework.

The first cross-sectional study of personality in older adults was reported in 1962 by Reichard. This study had an all-male sample, from which five personality types were identified. The men's personalities were categorized as follows: mature (stable, well-balanced, accepting of aging); rocking-chair (passive, somewhat dependent on others, voluntarily disengaged); armored (rigid, disciplined, individualistic, active, highly independent); angry (hostile, blaming others for declining abilities, unstable, fighting against social and physical signs of aging); and self-hater (blaming themselves, depressed, isolated). As may be deduced from the descriptions, the first three types (mature, rocking-chair, and armored) are positive adjustments, while the latter two (angry and self-hater) are malfunctioning types. It should be noted in this context that the disengaged individuals (rocking-chair) are not considered poorly adjusted, based on the study; this choice of behavior is considered a viable option and is not viewed as pathological.[19]

An important study that used this first categorization as a starting point was by Neugarten, Havinghurst, and Tobin.[20] They identified four groupings. The *integrated* personality functions well both internally and in society. The *armor-defended* personality is driven, striving for success. The *passive-dependent* personality and the *unintegrated* personality have pathological characteristics, which their labels suggest. The overall results of this study indicated that whether or not a person is active in older life or becomes disengaged depends upon personality characteristics most of all. As we have suggested earlier, a good adjustment in earlier life is a strong indicator of good adjustment in the later years. In general, this study came out on the side of activity rather than disengagement; the older individuals who remain connected to life outside themselves were far more likely to be satisfied.[21]

The identification of life-styles based on the above personality types was the focus of a study by Havinghurst.[22] The study was, however, relatively small, and it must be stressed that not all older adults can be identified by the life-styles given here. In addition, personality was found to be highly stable, and so it can usually be seen that these elders had the same types of personality in younger life that they had when they were studied as elders. The integrated personality may be "reorganizers" (engaged in a variety of roles and activities, replacing lost roles with new roles), "focused" (with interests centered on a few activities or roles), or "disengaged" (relatively uninvolved in social life). The armored or defended type may be "holding on" (attempting to continue midlife roles and activities) or "constricted" (fighting against aging by restricting social interaction to a few activities or roles). These positive orientations are followed by the less-desirable adjustments: the passive-dependent personality type may be "succorance-seeking" (dependent on attention and emotional support from others) or "apathetic" (passive, with little social involvement throughout life); and the unintegrated personality type has a "disorganized" life-style (unable to control emotions, behave consistently, or think clearly).[23]

A useful study that looked at the differences between men and women, identifying different life-styles as well as personality types based on sex, was reported in 1974 by Maas and Kuypers. This was a longitudinal study, with interviews from the individuals in their thirties and again in their seventies. Maas and Kuypers listed six life-styles for women (husband-centered, work-centered, group-centered, visiting, uncentered, and disabled-disengaged) and four for men (family-centered, hobbyists, remotely sociable, and unwell-disengaged). Many of the women partook of changing societal patterns and moved from being husband-centered to work-centered when they moved outside the house to employment; the men, by contrast, were relatively stable in orientation. Four personality types were identified for women (person-oriented, fearful-ordering, autonomous, and anxious-asserting) and three for the men (person-oriented, active-competent, and conservative-ordering). Unlike the life-styles, changes in personality were observed more often in men than in women. The conservative-ordering men tended to become even more conservative, and the active-competent men became less active with age.[24]

While arresting as a whole, the theoretical framework that described Type A and Type B behavior has not been studied systematically in elders. What studies do exist have suggested that Type A behavior is much less prevalent in elders, but this may be a group difference (i.e., cohort) rather than a change in orientation with aging.

In summary, therefore, in regard to both personality types and life-styles, the studies have shown through rather complicated categorization that elders are generally stable in personality, manifesting the same personality traits in older life that they manifested when younger. Some differences do exist that are subject to influence from the social environment, and overall, the individuals may become less active with age than they have been in the past. This raises once again the question of disengagement, which has been viewed by these studies as a legitimate and usually positive orientation for the elder. In general, however, the activity model is in current vogue as the life-style of choice for the elder.

### *Relationship to Information-Seeking Patterns*

The relationship between personality change versus continuity and information-seeking is rooted in the extent to which a person becomes disengaged or remains active. Certainly when the individual has less contact with the world exterior to himself or herself, there will be less chance to satisfy information needs. Conversely, a still-active elder will encounter many people by which his information needs can be met. This suggests that daily contact is a vital link to the outside world. It is possible, however, for the elder to keep a few close ties that satisfy informational as well as other needs. He or she may have particularly close ties with a physician, for example, or a child, and these people may see that the elder knows what he or she needs to know to function in society. A few close ties that satisfy needs would not be inconsistent with disengagement. In general, however, the greater one's mix of outside contact, the greater likelihood that informational, as well as other needs, will be met. Society has become so diverse that a few close ties may not be sufficient for information literacy.

### *The Older Adult Externally: Life Transitions*

As mentioned in the introduction, older adults do experience dramatic change in their lives; this change is frequently traumatic, with nothing in their preceding lives having prepared them for these inevitabilities. We will discuss three major changes with which at least a substantial minority must cope: retirement, death of a spouse, and institutionalization. All have implications for information-seeking and information-gathering.

### *Retirement*

Retirement is a relatively new phenomenon for elders, having become institutionalized with the advent of Social Security. Prior to this, older people were expected to keep working as long as they were able. The fact that many could not, due to health conditions, was the primary impetus for Social Security. The decision to retire is dependent upon a variety of life conditions: finances, pressure to withdraw from the work force, poor health, and, finally, attitudes toward retirement itself based upon satisfaction or dissatisfaction with one's work.

The availability of enough money to live comfortably is the single most important determiner in the decision to retire. Today a sixty-two-year-old can collect 80 percent of his or her retirement benefits from Social Security. This fact alone is a substantial one in encouraging early retirement. Complicating this picture is the fact that individuals up to age seventy who earn a substantial working income are penalized, in that their Social Security will be reduced. (At age seventy and beyond, one may earn an unlimited amount and still draw one's full Social Security.) But working in the opposite direction, to encourage continued employment, is the fact that after age sixty-five, an individual receives a bonus from Social Security for each year that he or she delays retirement. This latter incentive has not, to date, led to substantial curtailing of early retirement.

Individuals may be subtly encouraged to retire in order to make room for younger employees, although age discrimination is against the law. Elders cannot usually be forced to retire, because of legislation that precludes mandatory retirement. When older employees do face layoffs, they frequently choose retirement instead of other employment, which, despite the law, may be difficult to find.

Condition of health is another crucial determinant. In a study by the Social Security Administration, 65 percent of males cited poor health as their reason for retiring. Women were less likely to retire for this reason (38 percent). Because men live shorter lives than women, it is understandable that at retirement age their state of health would be a greater determiner. It is also possible that it is socially more acceptable for women to retire out of free choice.

Attitudinal factors also play a part in retirement decisions, especially since retirement is more and more viewed by society as desirable. One's job satisfaction is also influential, making disliked jobs more likely to be discarded. An aversion to retirement will delay the choice, but relatively few people now have this attitude.

Retirement means the loss of regular contact in an eight-hour (or longer) day with a variety of other people—a situation that can significantly influence one's information-seeking behavior. During the working life, one frequently functions in the world by turning to others for answers; the frequency with which this happens may go unnoticed until this daily support is no longer present. Not only is the "people contact" lessened, but information via the printed word may also be lessened; one does not, for example, have access to all those work-related memoranda and periodicals. The older adult who begins retirement must make an effort to stay current to the degree that he or she wishes, and this may not always be possible. Certainly information-seeking is likely to require more of an effort, and not a few elders will not know where to turn.

### *Widowhood*

Losing one's spouse is largely a female experience. One out of every seven or eight women over age eighteen are widows—ten million in all in the United States. By contrast, there are only 1.8 million widowers in the United States. There is some evidence to suggest that women make the adjustment better than men, but because women are much more likely to be forced into this situation, we will focus on their adjustment.

Losing one's partner means, of course, having to mourn the loss of one's significant other. The habits of a lifetime may be altered. Moreover, disruption occurs in the larger societal framework. Many of the couple's relationships may have been predicated on being part of a couple, and so these relationships at least undergo change, if they aren't broken. Other ties, such as those to the husband's family, may be lessened. Frequently the woman must adapt to living alone, something she quite possibly has never done before.

We have seen earlier that disengagement can lead to problems in information-seeking and -gathering, and even when the widow does not disengage, she will be at a disadvantage because longtime ties are frequently altered or even severed. Her emotional attitude may put her at a disadvantage as well. Grieving for the lost spouse may make her unreceptive to the overtures of family and friends who might otherwise assist her.

Death of a spouse is rated as the most stressful event on the Social Readjustment Rating Scale.[25] There is evidence, however, that long-term adjustment is remarkably good among elderly women. While older women are more likely to visit their physician in the year immediately after their loss, they do not visit more often in subsequent years.

We do have two large-scale cross-sectional studies of widows. Both were directed by Lopata.[26] The first consisted of 301 widows over age fifty—half over sixty-five. This study revealed that these women were leading quite independent lives; the vast majority either lived alone or were heads of households. They were not dependent upon others for their everyday needs, but reached out usually only for companionship rather than for various kinds of support. The most satisfied women were in better-educated, higher-class households. Women with little education and from the lower class, economically, were likely to be well adjusted only if their lives were stable. More education would thus seem to be a predictor of better adjustment, and this idea reinforces an assumption of this book: Knowing where to get information can make everyday living much better, in that problems are solved when the information is obtained. (Education presumably reinforces this.)

A second study enlarged upon the first and gave insights into the nature of the women's lives in some detail. In this study, it was found that the women's support systems were limited, and almost never consisted of institutional support. Children were named as the most important emotional support, but the highly independent nature of these women's lives suggested a degree of isolation from others.

Widowhood, as suggested above, may cause a reduction in the sources and kinds of information that one has. Not only is the spouse gone, but other significant others may be affected as well. The extent to which older people are isolated does not bode well for information transfer.

### *Institutionalization*

The cross-sectional figure of 5 percent of older adults who are institutionalized is, unfortunately, misleading. It does not give the likelihood, after age sixty-five, of some period of institutionalization before death. Indications are that the actual figure may be as high as 39 percent. This figure comes from a study by Vincenter, Wiley, and Carrington.[27] Institutionalization, therefore, is a likely occurrence for a significant minority of older adults at some point in their lives.

The quality of nursing homes is a matter of public concern and debate. Studies have shown that the highest ratings are held by those institutions in which staff feel that they have input as well as the resources that they need; and the physical appearance of the premises, the staff/resident ratio, and the breadth of service are also important. Typically, all of these factors are present at the same time.

There are a disproportional number of unmarried elderly persons in institutions, and usually the relative health of this group will be better than that of the married resident. This is due to the obvious reason that spouses usually care for each other as long as possible and so health is poorer upon entrance to an institution. Unmarried people need the institution sooner, having no one to care for them.

The personality characteristics of those who do best in nursing homes are disconcerting. It is the aggressive individual who shows little empathy for others who seems to function most optimally.[28] This can be explained in part by the fact that these individuals tend to be more independent, and therefore relate better to the impersonality of an institution. Upon reflection, one can see that the ability to assertively express one's needs may put one at an advantage in an institutional setting, and distance from others may be advantageous when death is a constant visitor.

We will discuss more fully the blight of the institutionalized in chapter 9. For now, it is sufficient to note that institutionalized individuals are usually highly dependent upon others for the satisfaction of all their life's needs, including information.

### *Summary*

We have thus seen that the older adult undergoes both internal and external change that influences and is influenced by his or her personality. Internally, changes are likely to be minimal in the wake of normal life developments. Only if pathology intervenes are the psychological changes severe. We are dealing, therefore, with a relatively stable core of personhood that adjusts in older life to the same degree that has been manifested earlier. External changes are evident in the primary life transitions most elders must make: retirement, death of one's spouse, and, for a significant minority, institutionalization. Again, if pathology does not intervene (and it usually does not, except in the case of institutionalization), then the changes are experienced, to perhaps a surprising degree, independently of support systems. Personality is the vital force that integrates the elder's world, influencing the decisions that he or she makes. Whether or not information-gathering and information-seeking patterns are disrupted depends in large measure on the degree of disengagement that occurs. And current thinking is that elders are better served by remaining active and involved with life around them.

## Notes

1. Barry D. McPherson, *Aging as a Social Process: An Introduction to Individual and Population Aging* (Toronto: Butterworths, 1983), 199.
2. Janet Belsky, *The Psychology of Aging: Theory, Research, and Practice* (Monterey, Calif.: Brooks/Cole, 1984).
3. K. Warner Schaie, "Age Changes in Adult Intelligence," in *Aging: Scientific Perspectives and Social Issues*, ed. Diane Stene Woodruff and James E. Birren (New York: Van Nostrand, 1975), 120.
4. Belsky, *Psychology of Aging*, 116, reporting Jack Botwinick and James E. Birren, "Mental Abilities and Psychomotor Responses in Healthy Aged Men," in *Human Aging: A Biological and Behavioral Study*, ed. James E. Birren et al. (Washington, D.C.: U.S. Public Health Service, 1963), 97–108.
5. McPherson, *Aging as a Social Process*, 201.
6. Ibid.
7. David A. Walsh, "Age Differences in Learning and Memory," in Woodruff and Birren, *Aging*, 129–30.
8. McPherson, *Aging as a Social Process*, 202, reporting Bennet Murdock, "Recent Developments in Short-Term Memory," *Quarterly Journal of Experimental Psychology* 18 (August 1966): 206–11.
9. Belsky, *Psychology of Aging*, 136.
10. Nancy J. Treat and Hayne W. Reese, "Age, Pacing, and Imagery in Paired-Associate Learning," *Developmental Psychology* 12 (March 1976): 119–24.
11. Ellen Langer et al., "Environmental Determinants of Memory Improvement in Late Adulthood," *Journal of Personality and Social Psychology* 37 (November 1979): 2003–2013.
12. Harvey C. Lehman, "The Age Decrement in Outstanding Scientific Creativity," *American Psychologist* 15 (February 1960): 128–34.
13. Wayne Dennis, "Age and Achievement: A Critique," *Journal of Gerontology* 11 (April 1956): 331–33.
14. Lewis Aiken, *Later Life* (Philadelphia: Saunders, 1978), 76.
15. Leon J. Epstein, "Depression in the Elderly," *Journal of Gerontology* 31 (May 1976): 278–82.
16. Bernice L. Neugarten and Karol K. Weinstein, "The Changing American Grandparent," *Journal of Marriage and the Family* 26 (May 1964): 199–204.
17. Erdman B. Palmore, "The Effects of Aging on Activities and Attitudes," *Gerontologist* 8 (Winter 1968): 259–63.
18. Bruce W. Lemon, Vern L. Bengston, and James A. Peterson, "An Exploration of the Activity Theory of Aging: Activity Types and Life Satisfaction among the Movers in a Retirement Community," *Journal of Gerontology* 27 (October 1972): 511–23.
19. Suzanne Kate Reichard, *Aging and Personality* (New York: Wiley, 1962).

20. Bernice L. Neugarten, Robert J. Havinghurst, and Sheldon S. Tobin, "Personality and Patterns of Aging," in *Middle Age and Aging*, ed. Bernice L. Neugarten (Chicago: University of Chicago Press, 1968): 173–77.
21. Aiken, *Later Life*, 84.
22. R. J. Havinghurst and Augusta De Vries, "Life-styles and Free Time Activities of Retirement Men," *Human Development* 12 (1969): 34–54.
23. McPherson, *Aging as a Social Process*, 211.
24. Ibid., 212–13, reporting Henry S. Maas and Joseph A. Kuypers, *From Thirty to Seventy* (San Francisco: Jossey-Bass, 1974).
25. Belsky, *Psychology of Aging*, 59, reporting E. K. Eric Gunderson and Richard H. Rahe, *Life Stress and Illness* (Springfield, Ill.: C. C. Thomas, 1974).
26. Helena Znaniecka Lopata, *Widowhood in an American City* (Cambridge, Mass.: Schenkman, 1973), and *Women as Widows: Support Systems* (New York: Elsevier/North Holland, 1979).
27. Letitia Vincenter, James A. Wiley, and R. Allen Carrington, "The Risk of Institutionalization before Death," *Gerontologist* 19 (August 1979): 361–67.
28. Barbara F. Turner, Sheldon S. Tobin, and Morton A. Lieberman, "Personality Traits as Predictors of Institutional Adaptation among the Aged," *Journal of Gerontology* 27 (January 1972): 61–68.

CHAPTER

# 4

# Sociological Influences

Life in the later years is usually characterized by great change. The degree to which successful social adjustment is made determines in large part the happiness or unhappiness of the later years. A particularly useful way of addressing change is to analyze the life situation of elders from the standpoint of the varying roles that they assume as the years go by. We will first examine this matter of roles in the later years within the framework of family dynamics. This will be followed by an in-depth analysis of work and retirement, including the economic situation of the elder; the physical environment and its effects, including change of residence due to health conditions (increasing dependency, disability, or institutionalization); and participation in religion, politics, and leisure-time activities. Much of the analysis is drawn from copious research cited and described by McPherson.[1]

## Roles within the Family

Research on the roles that adults assume within the family toward the end of the life cycle has been much less extensive than research on the younger years, although recently this lack has been partially redressed. Another drawback is the fact that the available research is largely descriptive rather than analytical. And, finally, not always has the research focused on the point of view of the elders themselves. But we want here to approach the subject, using the available research, in an analytical way from that point of view. (The points of view of the others in the family will be addressed only insofar as their views influence the elder significantly.)

An elder can assume various roles within the family: wife or husband, mother or father, aunt or uncle, grandmother or grandfather, widow or widower, sister or brother, and even, given our extended lifespan, daughter or son. These various kinship roles alone ensure that relatively few people will be without ties in their later years. But these ties undergo change that can be distressing, particularly at this time of life.

It is largely a myth that earlier generations lived, sometimes three generations at a time, in the same household. Laslett (1971) argued that the lifespan was much shorter; independence for young people was the norm (as it is today); many moved west from the East to take advantage of greater opportunity; and there was no compulsory retirement to create economic hardship.[2] Consequently, separate households were much more common than has generally been supposed, and shared premises probably occurred only when declining health made living alone difficult or impossible. Then, as today, however, extended families interacted frequently, providing social support and sometimes satisfying financial needs as well. In fact, today it is most common for at least one child to live within an hour's driving distance from the parents.

There have been changes both in the family demographics and in the social setting that affect the support provided by members of the family for one another. Now there are fewer children per family; childraising was completed earlier (only very recent years have seen a trend toward late-life parenting); and the married couple, because they live longer, can look forward to more years together as a couple after their children are grown. Socially, each succeeding generation has been better off than the last, freeing offspring from financial ties to family; each succeeding generation has been more mobile than the last; more women are employed outside the home; and, finally, there are additional governmental programs to assist the aging.

Despite the fact that these factors mitigate, to some degree, against close and supportive family ties, there is little evidence that elders are neglected by their offspring and others in their extended family. As we have noted, most commonly the elderly live within an hour's drive of at least one child. That elders are insufficiently cared for by unfeeling, selfish children is a corollary to the myth that earlier several generations lived together in the same household. It is largely because institutional care has arisen that these charges have been given fuel. We will address this issue subsequently.

### The Elder as Spouse

Elderly couples are likely to recoup the joy they shared before the arrival of their children—and the consequent responsibilities. Indeed, their joy may be greater than that which they experienced as newly-weds.[3] Of course, this does not speak well for the influence of offspring on the marital relationship. In more concrete terms, one can note that the peaks of happiness at the beginning and (relative) end of the marriage can be attributed to the similar life-styles of the pair. Both stages are adult-centered and child-free, both partners have more time to engage in activities together, and household responsibilities are more likely to be shared.

The point at which this greater camaraderie once again takes place is when the last child leaves home, thereby creating the "empty nest." It is more likely now than ever before that this will have occurred in the middle-adult years. (As such, this actual moment is not our focal point in the lifespan.) It should be noted, however, that contrary to myth, the transition in role is not perceived as particularly traumatic for most individuals. It is prepared for and sometimes awaited eagerly. Only the woman who has centered her life around her children must readjust her priorities.

Older married adults can enjoy high levels of satisfaction in a variety of marriage "types." Medley identifies three patterns that are relatively typical: (1) the husband-wife type, in which the relationship between marriage partners is paramount and all other relationships are seen as secondary to it; (2) the parent-child type, in which one partner is noticeably dominant and the other is dependent upon the dominant one (a common situation when illness enters the picture); and (3) the associate relationship, in which the marriage partners are friends but derive most of their satisfaction from other people rather than each other. Although (as indicated) circumstances may lead to the adoption in late life of a different pattern, it is much more common for a given type to have been in effect throughout the length of the marriage.[4]

Every marital relationship ends in a death (if not divorce or separation before that), and in most cases this is the death of the husband. Widowhood has sociological implications as well as psychological. (For psychological implications, see chapter 3.) There is usually little possibility for sociological integration prior to the actual point of a spouse's death. If the husband has been ill, in most cases the wife has been the caregiver and has been fully occupied in this role, with little or no opportunity to integrate socially with others. If death is sudden, there is even less likelihood that widowhood has been anticipated in any realistic sense. (There is one exception: if the wife is advanced in years and has seen many of her friends become widows.) Recent research suggests that the period of grieving may last far longer than had been realized. But the truth does appear to be that most widows eventually go on to live successfully in society as single persons. Coping is almost universally recognized to be easier for widows than for widowers. Possible reasons range from the greater domestic skills of women to the suggestion that women in general cope with grief better because they are required less often to mask their emotions.

### *The Elder as Sibling*

Relatively little research has been done on sibling relationships in late life, although it is estimated that 75–90 percent of the older population have a surviving sibling. There is some indication that the camaraderie that existed in the early years, and was abandoned when family demands were strong, may return in the later years (unless there has been rivalry or dissension). Female bonds tend to be particularly strong; i.e., sister-sister interactions are more common than brother-brother or sister-brother. Sister-sister bonds are particularly likely when both are widowed, and the sister-brother bond is likely to become stronger if the brother is a widower. (The sister may become a kind of surrogate wife, seeing that her brother has the domestic support that he needs.) All in all, sibling bonds have the greatest potential outside of parent-child bonds for necessary support in the later years.

### *Parent and Adult Child Bonds*

Parent and child bonds are in many respects the most significant in existence. The parent cares for the infant and young child, giving support when the child is unable to survive independently. These bonds are loosened, often with pain, when the child reaches adolescence and must separate emotionally and physically from the parent to assume independent living. When the young adult forms his or her own family (marriage and children), the ties to parents may become more egalitarian. Ultimately, when the parent is old, the adult child gives support in much the same way that he or she has received it.

Despite this common scenario, it is a myth that older adults are emotionally children again ("once an adult, twice a child"). While some dependence may be inevitable if health declines, elders generally champion independence, preferring their own households as long as possible, and, as is often stated, not wishing to be a burden on their children. There are some class differences. Some studies have shown that working-class parents are more likely to receive more help and to live with their children, whereas the middle-class (parents and children) are more likely to exchange gifts and money. The advantages of higher income are here directly reflected, as are the possible advantages of greater educational levels. The middle- and upper-class elders would seem better predisposed to remain independent of their children for longer periods of time. They are more likely to live at some distance, due to social mobility, but letter-writing and telephoning are commonplace substitutes to the face-to-face interactions that the working class enjoy.

There are also differences between male and female children with regard to the care and support of their parents. The male child is more likely to support financially, whereas the female child is more likely to provide direct service. It is also the female child who most frequently cares for the parent, if need be, in her home.

"Intimacy at a distance," to adopt Rosenmayr and Kockeis's term,[5] seems to be the choice, therefore, of both parents and children. Parents want adult children to live independently (i.e., separate from the elders), just as the elders did at their age. They want to interact yet remain independent, but they do expect assistance if it is needed. A recent study has suggested that parents may want more interaction than they have, but are willing to settle for what is given, due to their children's relative independence.[6] Very little research has been done on the quality of the interaction, but there seems to be a correlation between quality and quantity. The more often parent and child spend time together, the better that time is perceived in terms of satisfaction on the part of both.

### Grandparent-Grandchild Interaction

Most children have the opportunity to know a grandparent. At age ten, 90 percent of children have at least one surviving grandparent; by age twenty, the percentage has declined to 75 percent. Because of increased geographical mobility, however, face-to-face contact is less frequent than in earlier generations. The grandparenting that does occur is more likely to be done as a couple because of increased longevity.

Grandparenting is a highly personal and individual role, with relatively few norms to establish it. Only in the working class is the likelihood increased that it will be a "real" role, requiring integration of the grandparent(s) into the daily life as an extended family member. Otherwise, the grandparent is free to write his or her own script. The stereotypes of Grandpa taking a child fishing and Grandma baking cookies are less relevant today, although children may find that their grandparents tend to be more relaxed around them than their own parents are. Grandparents frequently are less demanding of their grandchildren than the parents are, since the parents may have substantial ego involvement in seeing the child succeed. There are advantages to grandparent-grandchild interaction in both directions—so much so that foster grandparent and grandchild programs have been set up, creating a relationship that helps both in the absence of the real thing.

### *Relationship of Role to Information Receipt*

In a theoretical sense, the more roles that an elder fulfills—spouse, sibling, parent, grandparent—the greater the likelihood that informational needs will be satisfied due to the multiplicity of individuals occupying that elder's world. The diversity is important because people at different stages in the life cycle and occupying different relationships to the elder will fulfill informational needs from different vantage points. Insight that cannot be gleaned from a given person can possibly be gleaned from another. Also, the type of bond makes a difference. Deep emotional need may be served by the spouse, but if one is concerned about the spouse's health, for example, and needs information as to how to help him or her, then the elder may *not* confide the depth of concern to that spouse, but instead turn to an adult child for practical assistance. In general, the more close relationships one is privileged to have, the greater the likelihood that needs, informational as well as other types, will be met.

## Work and Retirement

We have earlier (chapter 3) examined the psychological adjustment of older people to retirement. We will now address the sociological implications of the individual in the role of worker.

Retirement is a sociological phenomenon invented by industrialized society. Prior to the Industrial Revolution, men—if not women—

were expected to work until declining health forced an end to their labors, and only then did they turn as a last resort to their offspring or extended family members for financial and other support. Only in recent years has legislation (e.g., Social Security) made retirement under other, more positive conditions even possible for the great mass of humankind. Part of the rationale, in fact, behind the now-familiar Social Security was the fact that not all men (or women) *could* work until their deaths; illness and the loss of physical strength intervened. It is a measure of our progress that retirement has come to be viewed positively by the great majority of men and women; it is seen as something to which one is entitled, having earned the respite (and financial remuneration) from years of hard work. Although there is a great myth about the hazards of facing retirement, especially for professional men, the truth (supported by copious research) is that the vast majority of men as well as women make the transition smoothly and enjoy their final years, divorced from the workaday world.

Although the transition is generally smooth, definite stages have been identified through which one must navigate. Atchley suggests two stages prior to retirement: a stage in which one recognizes that retirement will eventually come and prepares for it by savings and pensions (i.e., "remote"), and the immediate time prior to retirement, in which one actively prepares by investigating the options, perhaps through formal pre-retirement sessions that are provided by one's employer (i.e., "near").[7] Following the actual day of retirement, there are five identified stages (also by Atchley): (1) an initial period of euphoria in which options are tried out (i.e., "honeymoon"); (2) a period in which the more realistic facts of retired life may impinge, negatively, such as reduced income or lack of meaningful activities ("disenchantment"); (3) the development of more realistic plans ("reorientation"); (4) the satisfying routine of the retired years ("stability"); and, finally, (5) the final coping with illness ("termination"). It will be obvious to the reader that not everyone goes through all the stages, and there is also great variation in when the stages may occur. Let us review first the years that immediately precede retirement, in order to determine what preparations are ultimately made. Then we will analyze retirement, per se.

### The Worker in Pre-Retirement

As we have noted in the earlier discussion on personality (chapter 3), individuals usually display continuity throughout the lifespan in regard to attitudes, values, behaviors, etc. How do these values affect the working life prior to the actual retirement decision? What are some of the more prevalent myths surrounding the older worker? (Does he or she become a less able worker in the final years of working life?) Unfortunately, most of the research has focused on the white male, and the extent to which these findings are applicable to the whole work force is debatable.

Work has been categorized in much research as the primary motivating factor in an individual's life. Its central focus ensures that it will determine, to a large extent, not only income but also social standing in the community. There is great continuity in the type of work which one does throughout the lifespan, either a sequence of jobs within a particular field of work or a sequence of jobs that require similar skills. Up to this time (there is some evidence that the pattern is changing), most individuals have displayed a stable work pattern, keeping the same or similar jobs throughout their working life and developing loyalty to the organization of which they are a part. White-collar workers consistently show greater satisfaction with their work, per se; blue-collar workers look more to the extrinsic values of work, such as income and friendships developed in the workplace. When work has been interrupted (by patterns of full-time employment, unemployment, part-time employment, and underemployment), individuals do not develop nearly the same commitment to a job or organization, as would be expected.

The meaning of work to the individual can change over a lifetime, and these changes can affect the choice of retirement and how satisfied the individual will be with his or her choice. Toward the end of the working life, it is possible that one will note a decline in satisfaction with career; frequently, this occurs because one must adjust to the fact that career aspirations may never be reached. This disenchantment can take the form of burnout (a period of little or no achievement, of running in place) or plateauing (a period of adjustment to the same level of employment due to a failure to advance). Also, people may just lose interest in continuing to do the same thing for long years, especially after there are no more promotions. Employers have introduced options to forestall this tendency: flextime and sabbaticals are two variations in the work schedule that serve to break up the tedium of a confining job.

Sometimes the disenchantment is too great, or, for other less identifiable reasons, one opts for a career switch in midlife. Obviously, the financial implications are great, and individuals without dependents are more likely to take this route. Usually one does not make this move for financial reasons, but instead because of a need to find work more intrinsically satisfying. Many individuals, in fact, will choose second careers that are distinctly less financially rewarding than what they had originally. The second time around, though, they will opt for greater freedom and flexibility. One must look long and hard before taking this route, as the disadvantages may outweigh the advantages. One needs to look at the "big picture," asking just what trade-offs one would be forced to take if drastic measures to switch careers or jobs were made. This is a problemmatical area because dissatisfaction does occur for many, and opting out is most frequently not the best solution.

As women have entered the work force in far greater numbers, there has been some attempt to study the relationships between their work and themselves. Typically, work occupies a central place in their lives as well. In midlife, in fact, it can become even more important than for men, in part because many women got a late start due to raising families. A number of factors influence the primacy of work in the middle and late years for women. Is the woman married? Women who are single, separated, divorced, or widowed are more likely to work out of economic need. In addition, health status, age of children, education, socioeconomic status, religion, and race all influence whether or not a woman will participate in the work force. New work patterns unique to women have been identified by Fischer (1979) as follows: (1) "nonentry," in which the woman is never employed regularly (full-time) after leaving school; (2) "delayed," where entry is postponed until midlife or later (often due to children); (3) "truncated," where a career is interrupted by marriage or children and never resumed; (4) "interrupted," where a woman leaves the work force temporarily and then returns; and (5) "full employment" or "dual career," where the woman works for her entire lifetime outside the home.[8]

Contrary to popular myth, there is little evidence to suggest that workers may decline in productivity with age. Any slowing down that does occur appears to be amply compensated for by experience. The research further shows that older workers are generally more satisfied with their jobs, showing little inclination to make a change late in life. Absenteeism is less for older workers as well, even in the face of the greater probability of illness. The few negative changes that do occur (such as slower reaction time, less muscular strength and endurance, some losses in sensory or cognitive skills) are readily compensated for. Basically, therefore, the myth of the failing worker in late life is just that—myth.

### *The Worker in Retirement*

Most older workers do not wait late to retire; the reasons for this have been analyzed earlier (see chapter 3). As long as relatively early retirement is the norm, society must adjust to a relatively large group of people who are no longer producing goods, so to speak, but who *are* using services. The economic ramifications of this situation can be great, especially when the number of retired persons increases (as will be the case about 2010, when the Baby Boom generation begins to retire).

Preparation immediately prior to retirement is largely an individual initiative, with very few older adults having access to formal preretirement programs. Those that do exist are largely group-oriented and financial in scope, and available primarily to white-collar males.

Historically, retirement in the United States has been mandatory. This was largely abandoned through recent legislation, but in actuality few older persons take advantage of the right to work indefinitely. Most workers retire voluntarily and, we might add, with positive anticipation. Retirement (as we have noted) is viewed positively by society, and the individuals directly involved benefit.

McPherson combines a multiplicity of studies to form the following list (here abridged).[9] The extrinsic factors that can lead to early retirement are: (1) high unemployment in society (when the chance of losing one's job and having to seek another makes retirement a viable option); (2) the option to receive partial (or total) retirement benefits at an early age; (3) a lowering or elimination of the requirement that one earn relatively little if pension or social security payments are to be received; (4) raising (or eliminating) the mandatory retirement age; (5) a forced horizontal or downward move in the job structure; (6) a norm within society that early retirement is socially acceptable; and (7) union demands on the number of maximum years prior to retirement. Personal factors that may lead to early retirement include financial security, decline in health, desire for a change in lifestyle, positive attitude toward retirement, supportive spouse and family, having few or no dependent family members, being employed in a physically demanding job, having little education, being marginally employed, making early concrete plans for retirement, and being dissatisfied with one's job. Predictably, the most influential factors are the degrees of one's financial security and the status of one's health.

Historically, it was felt that adjustment to retirement was the greatest single transition faced by men (as adjustment to widowhood was the greatest crisis for women), and that this transition was usually traumatic. In actuality, most men (and women) respond well to the transition and do not have major problems in adjusting. Major problems can include loss of income, declining health, and nostalgia for the job, but, of course, it is not inevitable that a crisis would necessarily result from any of these problems. Most older people, for example, adjust to lowered income by reducing their expectations; this does not seem to be a major problem for retired people, most of whom at this point in our history have adequate retirement income. Factors that point most often toward a satisfactory adjustment include an acceptable economic status and good health; others that have a positive bearing include a harmonious marriage and social support from one's family and friends;[10] a positive orientation to leisure or alternative pursuits (and, concomitantly, a reduced interest in one's field of work); adequate pre-retirement planning; and a level of social activity appropriately the same as before retirement.[11]

Women in retirement have been less studied. In the case of women whose husbands retire, it is felt that stress and adjustment may be necessary in the day-to-day life; after all, a husband may be present throughout the day, something never before experienced by the married couple. For women who themselves retire, there is conflicting testimony. Most white-collar women make a satisfactory adjustment, looking forward to retirement as does the typical male. Because women live longer, though, there are difficulties ahead that the male never knows. The most noteworthy of these difficulties is likely to be low fixed income, too small to live comfortably in one's final years. This is largely a problem that gets worse because of inflation, but it is also likely that the woman's pension, once she is widowed, is considerably less than what the two of them had as a couple.

### The Role of the Retired in the Economy

Retirees function in our society with economic benefits from largely three sources: government-based pensions (i.e., Social Security), private pension plans, and personal resources (e.g., the equity in a home). Generally, there is good news for the older adult in that he or she *is* generally able to maintain his or her position in the income hierarchy and to maintain a similar standard of living after retirement as before. The overall income will be less, but there are compensatory factors that work to the older person's advantage (e.g., owning one's own home so that mortgage payments are no longer necessary). Minorities suffer more than the white male, however, although the individuals who made the highest incomes just before retirement may feel the reduction more keenly. As noted, adjustments in expectations will usually come without great difficulty at the same time as the reduction in income, reducing the negative overtones considerably.

Women are at the greatest disadvantage because outliving their means can be a real problem that warrants early preparation. At the present time, it is common for older women never to have participated in the work force, or to have participated only erratically. Their situation in regard to retirement income is thus totally dependent upon the prior earnings of their husband.

### *Practical Implications on Informational Receipt*

As we have noted earlier in the section on the psychological effects of retirement (chapter 3), individuals who retire are out of the informational mainstream in many ways. The daily contacts at work are gone, and reading material that helps one to keep current may no longer be available. But even though this is true, it may not be germane to the question of informational receipt by the elder. His or her needs have changed, as one no longer employed; and the elder is no longer looking for the same sort of informational satisfaction that characterized the working years. Because the issues are different, the elder is not asking the same sort of informational questions of his or her world. No longer is there a need to keep up with the latest advances in the field to which one has devoted one's working life; while there may be a continued interest in keeping up, the necessity for a livelihood is gone. Moreover, the new informational interests themselves might be considered more "relaxed." Elders move at a more casual pace than do younger people who are caught up in the fast pace of modern life. The challenge is to develop contacts in a sociological sense that satisfy the informational needs that will come up. It is important not to become isolated from a changing world. Because the work contacts are no longer present on a daily basis, the elder would be well advised to seek out new relationships that can satisfy informational as well as other needs in the post-retirement phase of life.

### *Summary*

The societal response to the older adult in pre-retirement and retirement is not usually negative; not only is retirement viewed as desirable and as earned, but the worker is normally able to make a smooth transition, adjusting to the new life with few problems, even adjusting to lowered income with modest difficulty. Satisfaction in retired life is seen as the norm.

## The Role of the Elder in Relationship to Environment

The environment of older adults has been studied in recent years by gerontologists and sociologists who wanted to identify what the interplay between personal factors—health, economic situation, family conditions—and living situation might be. In general, the interaction between the two is much greater than is apparent at first glance. Individuals change roles throughout their lives, and as they change, their neighborhoods do as well; sometimes the neighborhood acts upon the individual, and sometimes the reverse is true. The research has sometimes had as its end point an attempt to identify optimal living environments for the older individual. We will analyze first the environment itself at the macro level (society), then move to a consideration of the individual within that environment at the micro level (one's dwelling itself). Finally, we will look at movement on the part of the elder—migration to and from various areas in search of the good life.

### *The Macroenvironment*

By definition, the macroenvironment includes the neighborhood, the community, and the geographical region in which one resides. One can derive considerable identity from these environmental surroundings, being hesitant to part with the familiar in old age. In general, the older adult patterns of choice in environment are stable; migration does occur with a significant minority, but "aging in place" is far more common.

Urban environments have been studied to a much greater extent than rural ones. And the conclusions drawn about rural environments frequently have been based on inferences drawn from the urban. In general, however, the following are characteristic of rural environments: fewer institutional services available, greater distances to travel to services and shopping, lower crime rate, lower per-capita income, less-healthy individuals (perhaps because average age is higher), distance from children greater, more widows, quality of housing lower because it is older, lower population density, neighbors at greater distance, and fewer alternative means of housing (e.g., apartments and retirement homes). Although some of these factors, because they reflect poor services, would seemingly point toward less satisfaction on the part of the residents, the truth is that they do not; people living in rural areas do not report less satisfaction with their lives than people who reside in urban areas. Fengler and Jensen attribute the satisfaction to more interaction with friends and neighbors, less fear (and incidence) of crime, smaller community size, and more informal support on the part of neighbors.[12] So the objective lowered quality of environment is compensated for by the intrinsic values of rural living.

The lack of transportation in the rural environment is one big disadvantage. Historically, transportation has been ranked among the greatest needs of elders; in order to maintain an independent life-style, the means must be found to navigate in the environment. If one cannot drive an automobile, he or she is forced to fit into the life-styles of those who do, or seek alternative arrangements. Public transportation is, alas, not always convenient or even available. Today more women have driving skill than ever before, and so this will be a diminished problem for elders as a whole in the future; only the old-old, because they frequently can no longer qualify for drivers' licenses, will be as restricted.

Crime is both a real and imagined problem for elders. Many report their fear of crime, perhaps due to their own perceived vulnerability rather than to any intrinsic danger. Elders, in fact, are victimized in fewer numbers than most other groups; this may be, in part, because many do not take risks that might put them in jeopardy. Larceny and burglary rates against the elderly are rising, however. And fear of victimization is a very real problem that restricts the movement of many elders; in some studies, as many as 50 percent of elderly people consider this fear to be one of their most serious problems.

### *The Microenvironment: The Elder's Dwelling*

The home is a major social center for the elderly person. Most have lived in the same place for years and feel comfortable and satisfied in that environment. Most own their own home. For the majority, this situation is fortunate, meaning that mortgage payments do not have to be met anymore, etc. But for a significant minority, upkeep of the house will eat into their fixed retirement income, causing a dilemma that becomes more acute as time goes by. In fact, studies have revealed that many older adults live in structures that are inferior to those in the surrounding neighborhood. Yet, most older adults prefer to maintain the status quo, although not all are able to do so. As this group ages, the lack of beneficial structure in the environment may jeopardize their health (old houses may have poorly designed stairs, old plumbing, and old electrical systems, etc.).

There are two continua along which choice of housing can fall: independent versus dependent living, and age-segregated versus age-integrated living conditions. Because the aging are a heterogeneous group, there is great variation in the pattern of choice. Findings have conflicted on whether age-segregated, or age-integrated, housing arrangements are preferred by elders. The reason for this is likely a variable based on characteristics of the sample. (Sampling is frequently done in age-segregated locales, because a large number of elders can be reached relatively easily.) We can conclude that many elders, but not all, do prefer age-segregated living arrangements. Frequently, age segregation occurs because individuals select homes at the approximate same time, and at the same age, and grow old together. In this sense, by growing old "in place," the age segregation is a by-product rather than being planned. Age segregation is also a viable planned alternative in housing, however, as witness the many retirement communities that exist nationwide. It is certain from the available evidence that the vast majority of the aging prefer independent living arrangements, choosing to be independent much more often than living with a child.

Institutionalization may occur toward the end of the life cycle; however, this is usually a much-feared alternative in living arrangements. Although less than 10 percent of elderly are housed in institutions at any given time, it is estimated that 25–75 percent are housed in an institutional setting during some part of the later years. Because it has become somewhat more socially acceptable to offer care to an elder in the form of a nursing home (although still controversial and not infrequently a source of great guilt on the part of the adult child), this alternative is chosen more often than ever before. If the financial and social situation of the elder is advantageous, and if children and other family members visit often, the environment will likely be acceptable; only poor economic and social conditions predispose an individual to substandard housing in institutions. This situation exists because governmental regulations are notoriously weak in policing such institutions, meaning that societal pressures must act to ensure a quality environment therein.

The shift to an institution in late life requires substantial adjustment by the elderly, adjustments that in some cases are not made easily. In fact, the death rates within one year of entrance to an institution are alarmingly high. While this is due in part to the elder's state of health, which has necessitated entry, there are concerns that the adjustment itself is not made readily, predisposing the individual to illness and death. Premature institutionalization should be avoided at all costs.

### *Migration in Late Life*

As we have noted, aging "in place" is a common pattern, but more and more older adults are choosing to uproot and begin life anew in a fresh environment. The increase in mobility and migration is due to such factors as urban renewal (and the displacement of elders who cannot afford to live in their old neighborhoods), more specialized housing planned and marketed to elders, changing norms that allow children to place their elderly parents in institutional settings, increased longevity and affluence that prompts one to seek warmer climes in the autumn years, and deteriorating housing or increased crime in the old neighborhood.

Despite the stereotype of the older adult moving south for retirement, the truth is that most moves made by elders are within the same county, not to mention state. Most moves of this type are made involuntarily, and are done so because of perceived inadequacies in the current environment (expensive housing, crime, etc.) Most long-distance moves are made by those between fifty-five and seventy years old, and a relocation is frequently precipitated by a transition point in life (e.g., retirement, death of a spouse, decreasing independence). Other reasons include a favored leisure life-style, a closer move to relatives, better climate, etc. A move, whether voluntary or involuntary, represents both a major opportunity and a challenge to the older adult.

### *Practical Implications for Informational Receipt*

If an older adult lives in company with others of roughly the same age and income level, he or she is likely to encounter the same informational problems as his or her peers. To the extent that anyone in the immediate circle finds an answer, the knowledge may be readily shared. Obviously, the more attuned to the environment and more information-rich the environment actually is, the greater likelihood that needed information will become available at the point of need.

Social service agencies can readily target areas that have high concentrations of older people, making the possibility of effective outreach more likely. While there may be advantages to having an adult child take care of problems that arise, the loss of independence mitigates against the attractiveness of this form of informational receipt. Adult children who are firmly a part of the society may, however, be in a better position to seek answers than an elder who (at the time) may be ill or depressed. Of course, if he or she is in good health, the elder will be much better situated to solve his or her own problems. You may recall that elders generally prefer to remain in heterogeneous communities, rather than age-segregated ones. This can be particularly advantageous, as there is a mix of individuals from whom knowledge (information) can be gleaned. There is always the chance that our fast-paced society has new solutions to problems that the elder has had no opportunity to learn. This is particularly a problem with governmental legislation and regulation actually designed to ease the life situation of elderly people. In such a case, assistance in working one's way through what can be an informational maze is welcome, regardless of where it originates. The environment, in a word, needs to be information-rich.

## Older Adults' Roles in Leisure Time

Leisure time in modern society has become more than the province of the rich and privileged. In fact, our whole attitude toward leisure has changed; we have moved beyond the Protestant ethic to acknowledge, at least, that individuals have the right to spend their time in ways other than constant productive labor. This change in attitude explains in large measure why retirement is anticipated and accepted by the larger society, as well as the aging themselves, as a positive and desirable time of life.

### *Labor Seen in Relation to Work*

Historically, the picture was far different. The individual could not choose to have leisure time; decisions concerning leisure were made by the leaders of society, which in many cases were religious leaders. Certainly leisure itself was not seen as a desirable end. With the Industrial Age, leisure continued to be seen in juxtaposition to work; i.e., leisure was defined as that part of life that was not spent working. Only in recent years has leisure, at least for the aged, been seen as something different from just the "opposite of work."

There is some indication, in fact, that leisure is now understood differently by retired individuals and by the populace in general. Retired persons are more likely to demand keen enjoyment from their leisure hours; people still in the work force may be more easily satisfied, in that they feel a reward and enjoy leisure just by the cessation of labor.

Three theories have been advanced to explain the types of leisure activities in which one engages. First, the "spillover" hypothesis suggests that leisure activities are similar to the activities in which one spends his or her working hours. Second, the "compensatory" hypothesis suggests that individuals choose leisure-time activities that are distinct from work activities, in an effort to compensate for lack in the regular work life. Third, a "neutrality" hypothesis suggests that there is little or no relationship between work and leisure activities, that neither choice affects the other to any great extent. To date, the "spillover" hypothesis has the most support from research, although there is still no overall consensus in the literature.[13]

### *Leisure in Retirement*

Relatively few individuals adopt new forms of activity in late life from those engaged in during early and middle adulthood. While there may be a period of experimentation just after retirement, most relax into their accustomed patterns (if health and fitness allow). The major forms of relaxation (leisure) for elders are as follows: socializing with friends and relatives, watching television, gardening, reading newspapers, and sitting and thinking.[14] Most activities, as may be deduced, take place in the home and are not community-based. Some are solitary activities.

Do older persons benefit from leisure activities? There is ample evidence to suggest that the more they are involved in such, the greater their satisfaction with life, and the better their adjustment to it. There may be a tendency to become active in other than purely leisure-like activities, too; social participation of all types may increase.

### *Volunteer, Political, and Religious Involvements*

Volunteer activities are more prevalent among the better-educated and those who have higher incomes. Beyond this, though, there are gender differences. Women are more involved in church, school, cultural, and hobby groups, and men are more involved in job-related, fraternal, sport, veterans', and other service associations.[15] There is a similar pattern of involvement over the life cycle, although in retirement there is a slight tendency for "joining" to increase. All in all, though, some people are, in fact, "joiners," and others are not (a speculation commonly made by laypersons).

Older people are disproportionately represented in the political process, a fact that is evidenced by any evening newscast. Incumbents often age in office due to the strong likelihood that they will win any given election. However, the general populace of older people may, as age advances, be less likely to vote, due to declining health or lack of transportation. Whether an elder is conservative or liberal may be more dependent upon cohort (i.e., group) differences than anything else; surprisingly, elders are perhaps more liberal than one usually assumes. There is some indication that elders are slower to change their minds on given matters than younger generations, however.

Religious participation is high among the elderly, although to some extent there is (perhaps surprisingly) less involvement than there was at an earlier age. (This may be due, in part, to increasing health problems.) In general, though, continuity in participation with younger years is apparent. More elders belong to churches than to any other institution, a fact that upon reflection is rather common knowledge.

### *Practical Implications for Informational Receipt*

It is apparent that leisure is an accepted part of life for elders now, as indeed it is for any age group. The decline of the work ethic is largely responsible for this positive attitude. The relationship between work and leisure has been much studied, with the "spillover" effect receiving most support. The extent to which recreational activities are similar to work activities would have a bearing upon the types of information sought and received in each instance. The more similar, the greater the likelihood that the same kinds of information will be gleaned from the environment. Volunteer, political, and religious involvements during one's leisure hours are an accepted part of many elders' lives. As we have noted earlier, the more active the senior individual, the more likely informational as well as other needs will be met.

## Summary of Sociological Influences

It is apparent that an older adult is influenced directly and strongly by what happens in his or her world, as viewed sociologically. This ranges from family ties and the elder's changing role within his or her family; to the important change from active working life to life in retirement, whether partial or complete; to changes in the immediate physical environment, which may include a change of residence; and, finally, to changes in the ways one spends his or her days in regard to religious affiliation and activity, political involvement, and other, more purely leisurely diversions. As we saw in our assessment of psychological influences on the aging process, the older adult who has been integrated into the community in his or her younger years will also adjust well to changes in such integration in late life. Many adjustments must be made in the course of growing older, but crises can generally be avoided if the social supports are strong enough. Familial ties thus become ever more important in the final years of one's life. What families cannot do, agencies in society frequently do in their stead. Sociologically, the elder will see much change in the declining years, but it is frequently true that those changes are beneficial and that the negative ones can be addressed effectively by a concerned family and a sensitive social network.

## Notes

1. Barry D. McPherson, *Aging as a Social Process: An Introduction to Individual and Population Aging* (Toronto: Butterworths, 1983).
2. Peter Laslett, *The World We Have Lost* (London: University Paperbacks, 1971).
3. Nick Stinnett, Linda Mittelstet Carter, and James E. Montgomery, "Older Persons' Perceptions of Their Marriages," *Journal of Marriage and the Family* 34 (November 1972): 665–70; Boyd C. Robbins and Kenneth L. Cannon, "Marital Satisfaction over the Family Life Cycle: A Reevaluation," *Journal of Marriage and the Family* 36 (May 1974): 271–83; Robert C. Atchley and Sheila J. Miller, "Older People and Their Families," in *Annual Review of Gerontology and Geriatrics*, vol. 1, ed. Carl Eisdorfer (New York: Springer, 1980), 337–69; Linda K. George, *Role Transitions in Later Life* (Monterey, Calif.: Brooks/Cole, 1980), 80.
4. Morris L. Medley, "Marital Adjustment in the Post-Retirement Years," *The Family Coordinator* 26 (January 1977): 5–11.
5. Leopold Rosenmayr and Eva Kockeis, "Propositions for a Sociological Theory of Aging and the Family," *International Social Science Journal* 15 (1963): 410–26.
6. Zena Blau, *Aging in a Changing Society*, 2d ed. (New York: Franklin Watts, 1981).

7. Robert C. Atchley, *The Sociology of Retirement* (Cambridge, Mass.: Schenkman, 1976), 63–71.
8. J. Fischer, et al., "Life-Cycle Career Patterns: A Typological Approach to Female Status Attainment," *Technical Bulletin* 8 (March 1979) (University of Alabama: Center for the Study of Aging).
9. McPherson, *Aging as a Social Process*, 386–87.
10. I. Krauss, "Individual Differences in Reactions to Retirement," Paper presented at the annual meeting of the Gerontological Society of America and the Canadian Association on Gerontology, Toronto, November 1981.
11. Anne Foner and Karen Schwab, *Aging and Retirement* (Monterey, Calif.: Brooks/Cole, 1981), 40; A. Matthews and K. Brown, "Retirement and Change in Social Interaction: Objective and Subjective Assessment," Paper presented at the annual meeting of the Gerontological Society of America and the Canadian Association on Gerontology, Toronto, November 1981.
12. Alfred P. Fengler and Leif Jensen, "Perceived and Objective Conditions as Predictors of the Life Satisfaction of Urban and Non-Urban Elderly," *Journal of Gerontology* 36 (November 1981): 750–52.
13. Gordon Staines, "Spillover versus Compensation: A Review of the Literature on the Relationship between Work and Nonwork," *Human Relations* 3 (February 1980): 111–29; John Wilson, "Sociology of Leisure," in *Annual Review of Sociology*, vol. 6 (Palo Alto, Calif.: Annual Reviews, 1980), 21–40.
14. Louis Harris, et al., *The Myth and Reality of Aging in America* (Washington, D.C: National Council on the Aging, 1975); Louis Harris, et al., *Aging in the Eighties: America in Transition* (Washington, D.C.: National Council on the Aging, 1981); Reinhold Schmitz-Scherzer, "Ageing and Leisure," *Society and Leisure* 2 (1979): 377–93; Miriam S. Moss and M. Powell Lawton, "Time Budgets of Oldest People: A Window on Four Lifestyles," *Journal of Gerontology* 37 (January 1982): 115–23.
15. J. Miller McPherson and Lynn Smith-Lovin, "Women and Weak Ties: Differences by Sex in the Size of Voluntary Associations," *American Journal of Sociology* 87 (January 1982): 883–904.

PART

III

# INFORMATION-SEEKING PATTERNS OF THE OLDER ADULT IN SOCIETY

In 1982 Schramm and Porter described a model of communication that is quite apropos of the model of information transfer being developed here. Our model is essentially and straightforwardly practical and factual in nature. Their model, in contrast, is exceptionally metaphorical and even picturesque. Their analysis compares our society's network of connected individuals and institutions to a telephone network or a computer system. The description reads as follows:

> We would see communication flowing over an almost infinite number of circuits. For any individual, most circuits, the most-used ones, lead to other individuals nearby. But there are some very long hookups: postal service, telephone, telegraph, and travel. Throughout the system are placed what in an electronic network we might call amplifiers. These are the mass media organizations—the schools, the libraries, the wire services, and other institutions and organizations—into which many circuits flow and which have the function of filtering out the input and producing a very large output of relatively few messages that go to many receiving points. Each of these institutions has its own internal communication network. On these networks and along the interpersonal chains of communications, we see smaller amplifiers: individuals who serve special functions in passing on communication—teachers, reporters, broadcasters, preachers, public information people, authors, advertising specialists, travelers, gossips, and many others.[1]

As we develop the next section, it will become apparent that Schramm and Porter have hit upon an apt way to illustrate informational transfer, although they do not use this terminology. As we describe the major ways in which information in our society is transferred, themes from the preceding extract will become apparent. First, though, in chapter 5, we will examine the transfer of information theoretically, drawing upon a number of theories in the social science literature. We will then turn in subsequent chapters to the factual description of informational transfer. We will examine both group-directed transfer via institutions as well as individual transfer via people. Although not always considered an "institution," the mass media are in fact essentially that (as well as being the primary means of group-directed informational transfer); mass media will be covered exhaustively in chapter 6. The component parts of "media" can be said to include books, periodicals, newspapers, television, radio, motion pictures, and the rapidly emerging world of computer technology (although such technology is not universally considered "media" at all). Chapter 6 will thus survey the media from the social scientist's perspective, signifying the importance of all of these means of informational transfer in daily living. The telephone will be covered in the chapter on media (because it is an electronic means of transferring information), but the simple asking for information on the person-to-person level will be exclusively covered in chapter 7, signifying the importance of daily interaction and personal contact with significant others. Finally, we will discuss in chapter 8 the primary institutions that transmit information to us—church/synagogue, school, library, and government agencies.

## Note

1. Wilbur Lang Schramm and William E. Porter, *Men, Women, Messages, and Media*, 2d ed. (New York: Harper, 1982), 90–91. Copyright © 1982 by Wilbur Schramm and William E. Porter. Reprinted by permission of HarperCollins, Publishers, Inc.

CHAPTER

# 5

# Theories of Informational Transfer via Media

The mass media are arguably the most influencial sector of our society today. Few would debate their pervasive nature, but this quality alone has perhaps made them difficult to study, too all-embracing to be scrutinized closely just in and of themselves. There are so many extraneous factors to be considered that research is likely to bog down of its own weight. Consequently, we will focus more on theories of mass media than on facts substantiated by research. We will begin with certain global theories that are relevant to our theme.

## The Functions of Media in a Changing World

One important aspect of the media that calls for study is their functionality in the modern world; i.e., what purpose do the various media serve in the lives of the individuals who view or hear them? This is a perspective that is quite important to older adults, and to us, as we peer into their world.

Leslie G. Moeller presents a well-defined analysis of media in the context most important to us. According to Moeller, the primary function of the media in society is to satisfy the public's need for information.[1] Although many people turn to the media for entertainment (and may think of the media in this context first), the entertainment function, in real terms, is clearly secondary to their informational value. Moeller asserts that modern industrial societies flourish on information; such societies thrive only if their citizenry is well-informed. In a nutshell, this means that citizens must know what is going on in the society, a need that Harold D. Lasswell calls "surveillance of the environment."[2]

There are three major phases to information via media: (1) day-to-day information that allows one to function in society (i.e., "instrumental" news, such as when taxes are due); (2) the updating of individuals on developments, changes, and needs in the society (e.g., the daily newscast); and (3) warnings about imminent threats and dangers (e.g., changes in the weather, hijackings, etc.). Certain needs within the individual are also satisfied by being well-informed. These factors, as delineated by Moeller, include the following: (1) personal esteem may be higher if one is always up-to-date on what is happening in the world; (2) individuals will have something to share with friends when they know what is current; and (3) an individual's innate thirst for knowledge is in part satisfied by keeping current.

An individual's need for news interpretation is met by media commentators on the national and international scene. Lasswell termed this function "correlation." The right kind of commentary can lower one's anxiety in the face of threatening events; this is a function that should not be minimized in our conflict-ridden world. Yet, there is a converse to this. The media's "hype" is a concern that is being noted more and more in the media. (In this, as in other matters, we look to the media to analyze themselves.) When the media have focused on one dramatic issue to the exclusion of others, the impact upon people's lives can be negative in that the trivial or even the terror-filled is sensationalized. And older adults are the victims as often as anybody else, perhaps more so, if other channels for information are limited.

Another study that focused on somewhat different ways of analyzing similar data was conducted by Bliese. In it, the functions of the media were evaluated by interviewing 214 individuals and twelve groups of people of eight to thirteen persons each.[3] Bliese identified ten functions:

(1) To supplement or substitute for interpersonal interactions;

(2) To gather content for interpersonal interactions;

(3) To form and/or reinforce self-perceptions and to gather information about societal perceptions of various groups of people;

(4) To learn appropriate behaviors (including age-appropriate ones);

(5) For intellectual stimulation and challenge (e.g., game shows);

(6) As a less costly substitute for other media (e.g., television news instead of a newspaper);

(7) For networking and mutual support;

(8) For self-improvement (e.g., exercise programs, language lessons);

(9) For entertainment;

(10) For "company" and safety.

There are many extremely relevant ideas, contained in this research, to our theme of informational transfer. In light of the importance of this research to our present theme, we will summarize Bliese's findings in some detail by discussing each finding in turn.

To supplement or substitute for interpersonal interactions is a function that immediately brings to mind the controversial disengagement hypothesis as well as the substitution hypothesis. Disengagement (see chapter 3) suggests that it is virtually inevitable that as people age, they will "disengage" from the society of which they are a part. The substitution hypothesis, as its name suggests, says that older persons will substitute communication via mass media for interpersonal communication when the latter is unavailable or difficult. Absolutely no older adult in Bliese's sample related that he or she *desired* disengagement; this finding further questions whether disengagement usually occurs. On the other hand, Bliese's sample supports the substitution hypothesis: 89 percent of her subjects engaged in substitution all or part of the time. (Forty percent used substitution occasionally; 32 percent, moderately; and 17 percent, extensively.)

Although the subjects acknowledged using mass media to substitute for personal interaction, a full 93 percent expressed moderate to extreme dissatisfaction over this state of affairs. A particularly poignant statement by a ninety-three-year-old woman illustrates their attitude: "I watch a lot of television and listen to the radio because I have no one to talk to. All my friends are dead and the relatives I have left don't care. But every time I turn the set on it reminds me that I have no one and that is very depressing. Sometimes I don't bother because I don't want to be reminded of my situation."

To gather content for social interaction (i.e., what to talk about) is obviously a more satisfying function of the media, one that may not be readily apparent. Forty-three percent of the sample used media in this way. Both specific and general information-gathering were used: "specific" might include looking at a popular television show that one's friends might watch; while "general" might be a way to keep current with the news. This function of the media is a reminder that most older adults want to remain knowledgeable about their world; as we have noted, the individuals in this study resist the idea that they would want to disengage from it.

To form or reinforce self-perceptions and to gather information about societal perceptions of various groups are related functions that have been documented by considerable literature. The literature sometimes links television and film characters to stereotypical examples of people in society. Although none of the participants in the study spontaneously related this as a function of the media for them (the responses in the interviews were open-ended), they did offer statements that expressed extreme displeasure with the negative portrayal of the elderly in the media. This is a common criticism of the media that any layperson would recognize as a problem. Everyone in the sample agreed that the effect on his or her own self-image was negative. Although the aging did not agree with the stereotypes, they had to fight against finding any validity in the negative portrayals of elders as useless, infirm, disagreeable, senile, and a burden. Obviously, elders would like to see more sensitive and accurate portrayals of themselves in the media. One aspect of their appeal for realism was the fact that they also believed that younger people are affected by this negativism. Finally, they requested more programs for and about older people, a request particularly pertinent to our central focus of informational transfer. More programs expressly for and about older people would considerably increase the potential for information-gathering on the part of older adults.

The media also serve to teach appropriate behaviors. Given the situation described above, however, there is limited possibility for vital and upbeat elders to see themselves in TV programs. Yet, 73 percent of the sample said that they followed advice given about appropriate role behavior, etiquette, and relations toward others. Given the negative stereotyping, however, we may wonder if this is helpful information for older adults, or if it may mislead them into unwittingly reinforcing negative stereotypes.

Intellectual stimulation and challenge are another surprising function of the media found by older adults. To understand this, we must recognize the pervasive fear among elders that they may lose their intellectual prowess. There is widespread folk belief, not supported by science, that stimulating the mind lessens the likelihood of senility. Many elders, for example, play against the players in TV quiz programs.

Selecting inexpensive media as a substitute for more costly media was a favorite action. Television, in particular, was used in this way: many "wait for the movie to come on TV," perhaps to save money or, more often, because it is more comfortable to view the movie in their own homes. In urban settings, this at-home activity also keeps one from going out on a perhaps-dangerous street at night. Some use radio and television news instead of buying a local newspaper, and letter-writing is even (perhaps rarely) used as a substitute for the telephone. In regard to printed material, which can be expensive, some elders shared periodicals with friends or read at the library instead of buying books. "Senior citizen" discounts were also highly popular.

The telephone is an important tool for networking and mutual support among the aging. Fully 97 percent of respondents felt that telephoning was as good or better than a visit; in some respects, it is superior (an idea expressed by some) because neither one's self nor one's home need to be presentable in order to engage in a telephone chat. Many use the telephone as a way to be sure that another is still in good health and not in need of assistance. Bliese felt that the telephone was important in maintaining cognitive functioning and psychological health because feedback and emotional support are what one receives while engaging in a telephone conversation.

Fifty-one percent of Bliese's respondents used the mass media in some way for self-improvement or education. This might range, for example, from television exercise programs and self-help programs (e.g., cooking, carpentry, etc.) to print sources that are read for educational purposes. In addition, many listened to music not just as a background accompaniment but as a way of learning something. Twelve percent telephoned a recording (e.g., a medical information service) for information they needed for everyday living.

Media for entertainment are as important for the aged as for anyone else, and virtually everyone in the sample used the media for this purpose. The rates of use ranged from twice a week to almost constantly. Emmert and Donaghy, in highlighting this function, make the point that even in "news"-papers, there is frequently much of purely entertainment value, e.g., comics, sports, movies, restaurant reviews, cooking tips, etc.[4] Moeller argues that the line between information and entertainment is so blurred that one cannot easily distinguish where one ends and the other begins.[5]

Finally, the media were used for "company" or for safety in the house. Many elders are fearful for their own safety and use the noise of a radio or television to ward off intruders; this was done both when the elder was out of the house as well as when he or she was at home. Police statistics do indicate some additional deterrence from a break-in when a radio or television is on in an unoccupied house. This function is akin to the "tranquilizing" function that Emmert and Donaghy describe,[6] although the point of view is not quite the same. "Tranquilizing" implies that the soothing nature of the background media will relax any person who is listening, a slightly different slant from Bliese's on the use of the media for "company."

There are other uses for the media in addition to information, interpretation, and the ten functions that Bliese identified. Specifically, as identified by Emmert and Donaghy (1981), these include an economic function, socialization, marketing, social change, social style, and "watchdogging." Let us examine these six functions individually.

In serving an economic function in our society, the mass media affect elders as much as anyone else. If the media did not make a profit, they would not long exist in the forms that we know them. Certainly, then, their need to make money dictates to a great extent what we will read or view. Even public radio and television are influenced by the economic motive, because much of their success is attributable to offering programs that will receive voluntary funding from the public.

The socialization function of the media serves to unify the society. It provides a common base of norms, of values, and of collective experience. Certainly television comes most frequently to mind in this regard, but radio served that function almost as powerfully a generation ago (and may still), and newspapers have fulfilled this function for far longer. In socialization, individuals learn "how we do things," and this in itself goes a long way toward explaining the unifying aspect of the media.

The marketing function is akin to the economic, in that advertising through the media is a major factor in the smooth operation of our consumer-driven economy. Advertisements influence consumers without their being fully aware how much (therefore serving an informational role unconsciously).

Another important but controversial role of the media is in initiating social change. Although nearly everyone who comments upon the power of the media touches on this aspect, few would assert that it is altogether a good thing. Many would say that the media should not attempt to engineer social change, but should be only transmitters of information on socially relevant happenings. But the line blurs, and the transmitters of the news by their choices also influence what will be seen as important to show. Demonstrators time their action for the camera, and if the camera were not present, the demonstration sometimes would not even come off. The tone in which information is conveyed serves to create a social style that has influence on the greater society. A rational, thoughtful commentary heard over the airwaves will suggest a much different orientation to the citizenry than will a shrill, outraged voice. The media are well known for watchdogging for the public interest. There could be no better example than the Watergate issue in the 1970s. In a similar way, the media also serve to safeguard civil liberties. The media also frequently provide a framework for the day, from the morning paper to the ten o'clock news. This provides a routine or ritual for the individual that goes beyond the transmission of the information itself.

In summary, it should be pointed out that the various types of media serve these functions to different degrees, some even more than we recognize consciously. Certainly the profit motive dictates to a great extent what we will read or view. As we have noted, even public radio and television are influenced by economics, because much of their success comes from offering programs that will receive voluntary funding from the public. No single medium can do all, or as equally well as other media.

All of the researchers we have highlighted—Moeller, Bliese, Emmert, Donaghy—support different theses about the role of the media in lives of people. Taken together, they give a sufficiently all-inclusive pattern for media in society that we can postulate that all people, including elders, cannot but be affected by the media's pervasive influence. It is not for us to say whether this is good or bad; it simply is a given. If we had to take sides, though, few of us would harken back to the days of less-available information, although we might take issue with the manner in which information is imparted. This brings us to the next task in an analysis of the transmission of information via the media—a delineation of the main ways in which information is imparted.

## The Media as the Shaper of Information

As we indicated above, in noting that demonstrators wait for the camera to demonstrate, we pointed toward a major effect that the media have in our culture. In earlier generations, religion was the principal shaper of human society; after Darwin, society came to be shaped by the view held by science. Now we might well consider that the mass media serve this function of shaper of opinion; unlike religion or science, however, there is no single ethos undergirding this pervasive influence. We have become a society that looks to the thrill or experience of the moment, the "hot" topic, as a shaper of our culture. Whatever the media turns their attention to rapidly becomes a "media event," which reigns until the next attention-getting event happens. Event follows event in a dizzying whirl, and we then say that the "media made too much of it." Snow suggests that this is not just a matter of people within the media industry exerting their personal influence; it is a strategy and consciousness that permeates society as a whole.[7] This climate for generating information can be particularly troublesome for elders, who remember a time when life rolled by much more smoothly, and the values of the society were firmly in place. In the next chapter, we examine each of the types of media in some detail, noting the degree to which the particular characteristics of each type affect the larger society of which elders are a part.

## Notes

1. Leslie G. Moeller, "The Big Four Mass Media: Actualities and Expectations," in *Beyond Media: New Approaches to Mass Communication*, ed. Richard W. Budd and Brent D. Ruben (Rochelle Park, N.J.: Hayden, 1979), 19.
2. Budd and Ruben, eds., *Beyond Media*, 20, citing Harold D. Lasswell, "The Structure and Function of Communication in Society," in *The Communication of Ideas*, ed. Lyman Bryson (New York: Harper, 1946), 37–52.
3. Nancy Wood Bliese, "Media in the Rocking Chair: Media Uses and Functions among the Elderly," in *Inter/Media: Interpersonal Communication in a Media World*, ed. Gary Gumpert and Robert Cathcart (New York: Oxford University Press, 1986), 573–82.
4. Phil Emmert and William C. Donaghy, *Human Communication: Elements and Contexts* (Reading, Mass.: Addison-Wesley, 1981), 361.
5. Moeller, "The Big Four Mass Media," 21.
6. Emmert and Donaghy, *Human Communication*, 363.
7. Robert P. Snow, *Creating Media Culture* (Beverly Hills, Calif.: Sage, 1983), 7.

CHAPTER

6

# The Transmission of Information via Mass Media

We will focus in this chapter on the major means of transmitting information to the aging in our society: books, periodicals, newspapers, television, radio, motion pictures, and (increasingly) computer technology—means for transmission which can be, as a whole, termed "media." The telephone will also be considered; although not usually considered part of the media, it is an important electronic means of transferring information person-to-person.

## Books

Certainly in an examination of those media that satisfy information need, we cannot overlook the book, that most heralded of creatures. As the mainstay of libraries, which themselves are viewed as repositories of information, the book still reigns supreme. Even in this era of computer technology and "paperless information," few seriously question the longevity and the future of this format; the book satisfies informational need in fundamental ways that will remain, regardless of what other formats emerge in our technologically oriented society. After all, one doesn't "cuddle up" with a computer (despite the prospect of new, flexible and portable screens, and including the fact that hackers derive considerable pleasure from their hours before the monitor). The ease with which this format is handled is an obvious plus, whether the book itself is a dimestore novel read for pleasure or the most scholarly treatise on the shelves of a research library. We will examine separately the use of books for popular reading and then delve into the use of books (actually frequently "monographs"), which are the mainstay of the academic researcher or student.

### *Popular Reading*

The image of the older library patron, still active and intellectually alive, who visits the library on an almost daily, or at least weekly, basis and checks out an armload of books is a popular image and one that delights the public librarian. Finally, the elder has the leisure to satisfy his or her intellectual curiosity, to read just for the fun of it, or, conversely, to set intellectual challenges in reading that were perhaps thrust aside during more active years. Of course, this is a stereotype, but perhaps it is a more favorable stereotype than we frequently find of the aging.

In recent years, many public libraries across the country have adopted an idea articulated by Robinson: provide reading that the public truly wants (with checkout records the criteria).[1] This idea, along with an attempt to copy a popular bookstore's image (and its method of displaying books), has revolutionized public libraries. As a result, the old stereotype of a massive structure with books neatly on shelves, presided over by a stern librarian, has fallen by the wayside, and public libraries as a whole have observed a resurgence in popularity unmatched in earlier years. As the former repository of the culture of a society, perhaps public libraries have now lost something, but few librarians of the current generation would go back to what once was. Fulfilling a need for the society of which it is a part has long been a credo of the library, and few would argue that this mission is not being carried out currently, albeit in different ways from the past.

### *Scholarly Research*

The libraries of colleges and universities are usually the repositories of materials studied for research purposes. (Private collections are, of course, still a necessity for many scholars.) Whether one is a harried undergraduate trying to prepare a term paper under deadline pressure, or a renowned scholar with a blissful sabbatical to devote to intensive study of a lifetime interest, the shelves of libraries are typically absolutely pivotal to the task at hand. In the current backdrop of an information explosion, there are numerous considerations. How does a given library get "enough" of the voluminous material available? If "access" via interlibrary loan is stressed, how can the turnaround time be made rapid enough to make such loans a suitable alternative? How much of the book budget will be consumed by rapidly spiraling costs for serials?

There are questions for publishers as well. Can books come out rapidly enough to have a real impact, or will periodicals and, increasingly, electronic communication become the way for scientists (in particular) in the years ahead? The old answers no longer serve, and the use of the book for scholarly research is undergoing change in our rapidly evolving scholarly environment.

## Periodicals

Unlike newspapers (to be discussed subsequently), periodicals vary by subject area and are therefore self-selected by readers interested in different slices of life. Periodicals are officially classified as either journals (scholarly material) or magazines (popular reading). They differ widely in use. Journals are research tools for the student or scholar, and articles to study are typically selected from indexes or bibliographies. Magazines, in contrast, are chosen by the average person for leisure reading that is typically cover-to-cover. Beyond this, the appearance differs radically as well. Journals have diagrams and charts, but few pictures, and those that do appear are usually in black-and-white. Magazines, in contrast, are a kaleidoscope of colors; illustrations abound, particularly in advertisements, and may even overshadow the written material. There are, as we have implied, few periodicals that have mass appeal. Even the ones that do exist are written for a specific market, as, for example, is *TV Guide*.

What influence do periodicals have upon the reader? Typically they have widely different effects, depending upon the degree of interest that has attended their reading. It is likely that the periodical was either read with great interest, attentively (the usual case for a journal); or, just the reverse, it has been used to pass the time in casual reading (more common for magazines, but not exclusively). The reader has likely been reading either for information or entertainment, and the two purposes likely dictate the degree of attention that he or she has given to the reading. For our purposes, of course, the informational reason is the most germane. It is in informational reading that the concept of *commitment* becomes important, as we will see below.

Readers choose specialized periodicals either because of an already-developed interest or a desire to learn more about the given subject. Usually the reader is or has the potential to become actively involved in the subject of the periodical. If it is a photography magazine, for example, and the individual isn't an avid photographer yet, it is very likely that the reader hopes to find him- or herself out buying a fancy camera someday—sooner more likely than later.

A reader of periodicals is in a better position to critically evaluate the information, because he or she does develop a certain expertise in the subject. This means that, from an evaluative viewpoint, periodicals are more susceptible to response from their readers than many other media; if the information is false or misleading, the reader will know it. (This is in contrast to television, which must appeal to a mass audience and may sensationalize the more negative aspects of our society.) Along with this interest comes a commitment to the periodical itself, because the reader who finds interesting information once is likely to read future issues for the same type of information. Subscriptions ensure that one has a say in what the periodical will turn out in the future; if the quality declines, the library or the individual will "vote" with the pocketbook and cancel the subscription. This ensures accountability on the part of the management of the periodical and serves to keep the periodical turning out the type of information that continues to draw its particular class of readers.

## Newspapers

When people think of a "media event," they may think first of television, but most certainly the second tool of the media to come to mind would be newspapers. Newspapers have a long and glorious past in our nation, with people relying primarily upon this print form of media for a recitation of the events large and small that have shaped our culture. Despite television's dominance of all media since 1950, the circulation (60 million) and the number (about 1,750) of newspapers have remained fairly constant.[2] The decentralized nature of newspapers ensures that the culture of large and small areas will be represented in print form. Indeed, the community newspaper serves as a microcosm of its area. Snow presents a thorough analysis of newspapers, reviewed below.

### *The Role of Newspapers*

Reading the daily newspaper is a ritual for many people. It serves as the backdrop for other routines, such as eating breakfast or riding the train or relaxing in the evening with a drink. It is a stereotypical idea that elders are more prone to such rituals than other people; in actuality, the only distinction may be the number of years in which one has engaged in a given ritual. For elders, therefore, newspapers have always been a part of their lives, and so the ritual aspects may be particularly strong. Reading the paper is symbolic of doing something useful rather than just wasting time. From an analytical standpoint, newspapers can be important in an individual's life as a standard of self-reference; being a "newspaper reader" implies a serious attitude toward life and an admirable awareness of the outside world. It can be postulated that this feature of bringing in the outside world is a motivator for elders, who are usually dissatisfied to be viewed as desiring disengagement from other people. Reading the daily newspaper would be one small tangible indication that the mind is still alert, the senses keen, and the orientation focused on the outside world.

Part of the history of the newspaper is its function as a community watchdog. Many papers have some version of this tradition as a slogan, frequently appearing on the masthead. Newspapers have been crusaders of the public's right to know; crime waves and government corruption are frequently exposed first on its pages.

The newspaper's role as the source for information and leadership in community crises is akin to watchdogging. A relatively recent example is the Iran-Contra Affair and an earlier pivotal case was the *Washington Post*'s investigative journalism into Watergate. The fact that leading newspapers in the country broke these stories illustrates the primacy of this role among the newspaper elite. The role of investigative journalism itself has been enhanced since the Watergate era; many small newspapers do their own digging into local issues and therefore make a substantial impact upon their communities.

Unlike a generation ago, most newspapers today are controlled by conglomerates. Another startling change is the fact that many media chains now have diversified their operations outside of the information business as well as within. Whether or not such changes will lead to a decline in watchdogging and investigative reporting remains to be seen.

### *Reading the Newspaper*

The newspaper is a compendium of far more than news. Advertising takes up fully 60 percent of its space, but the way in which newspapers are used in daily life ensures that readers will not object. Indeed, some readers buy the paper *for* the ads. Readers can browse the pages (unlike a captive television audience) to determine the best prices for categories of items that they wish to buy. This attitude is a bonanza for newspaper owners, as 90 percent of their revenue comes from advertising.

We do not know the answer specifically for elders, but we do have some indication of what readers in general read. A widely utilized market survey from the early 1970s listed what were perceived to be surprising figures: The most widely read stories were accidents and disasters (39 percent of readers), letters to the editor (35 percent), crime (33 percent), human interest (33 percent), and advice columns (32 percent).[3] At that time, newspapers devoted relatively little space to some of these items, but in the decades since, most have expanded coverage to more accurately fit this profile. (Human-interest stories on the front page, for example, are now commonplace.)

More in-depth coverage of news events, including interpretation of those events, is the rule. Newspapers and news magazines are now the only media that offer extensive commentary on the national and international scene. In contrast to television, which headlines the stories, newspapers' detailed account, and, in recent years, ample analysis give the educated reader something to absorb. As the average educational level of the population increases, this feature will become more and more attractive. There are also, for the reader on the run, columns that spotlight the major news of the day. Newspapers include their share of entertainment reading as well, though. The percentage of the paper that consists of syndicated column material is on the rise; this includes advice columns, book reviews, comics, crossword puzzles, etc.

As we can see, therefore, newspapers are a mainstay of life in our society, and this is just as true for most elders as it is for anyone else. They are a daily companion to which one turns in almost ritualistic fashion. As an imparter of information about the world in which we live, they are unsurpassed in regard to current events, and are highly important for other sorts of information as well.

## Television

Snow's analysis of the impact of television is as compelling as his analysis of newspapers. In his view, television has been studied extensively as a modern technological phenomenon capable of eliciting profound social change. Indeed, many changes have already been documented. The impact of television on the aging has been researched primarily from two directions: television's negative and stereotypical depiction of the aging, and the impact on the elderly of using television as a substitute for social interaction. Both types of research have uncovered negative implications for the elderly. The realization that television stereotypes in a negative fashion is disheartening, and the finding that the elderly may use television as a substitute for human involvement is equally unfortunate. Yet, we must look into this research for a clearer understanding of what it may be telling us. From there, we can speculate about what better uses of television might exist for the aging.

Actually the fact that television stereotypes the elderly is no different from what it does for any age group: stereotyping is the way in which situation comedies, police dramas, soap operas, etc., are able to tell a story convincingly in the relatively brief time slot dedicated to the given program. By resorting to stereotyping, the television writer is able to make a "sound-bite" statement that viewers can readily understand because they will fill in the missing characterization by the elements known to be a part of any given stereotype. This saves time, something that is in short supply with the typical half-hour and hour program. Stereotyping itself is thus a by-product of the medium of television itself. Yet, the fact that the stereotype for the elderly is largely negative is a cause for concern. Not only are younger people influenced by this image, but elders are also influenced, albeit involuntarily. Elders have been quoted as resisting the stereotype when viewing television, but nevertheless are depressed by it. They may realize that the negative image is wrong, at least to the point that they and most of their friends do not fit the stereotype. But younger people may not even question the image, because their views of the elderly may be almost totally shaped by the individuals depicted on the screen.

What is this stereotype? Davis characterizes it as follows.[4] When elders appear in television programs, they are much more likely than younger groups to be depicted as villains or as victims. There is a stronger tendency to depict women in this light than men. Most individuals who are older are not seen as happy or productive, capable of taking their place in society. Moreover, the situations that are depicted in television are not central to the life of an aging person; most programs do not address issues with which they are concerned, and as a result, it is very rare that the main character(s) is an older woman. Notable exceptions to this are the four main characters (all women) in the situation comedy "The Golden Girls," and Angela Lansbury in

"Murder, She Wrote." It is heartening to note this change, and we can speculate that perhaps the stereotype will change as time goes by. These exceptions perhaps indicate that more shows will be developed that depict elders in a more favorable light. In part, this is coming about because elders are beginning to be a strong consumer group, and television understands this reality via its advertising revenue. As consumer power grows, sponsors of programs will seek those shows that address the needs of their buyers; we will then see a change in the content of programs. More older people will be depicted, and it is also likely that the image will change. Sponsors may feel that elders are more likely to buy their product if the program that they are sponsoring is kinder to the elder, or, at the least, does not turn him or her off by the depiction.

Older adults are frequent viewers of television, as is the rest of society. Years ago, De Grazia's survey research found that watching television was the most frequent activity named by his sample.[5] And there is also some indication that viewing increases with age. Much has been written about television watching as a poor substitute for human interaction, an activity in which the elderly engage because of insufficient contact with other people.

The reasons for television's popularity, according to this thesis, are highlighted by Davis.[6] It gives the "illusion of contact" with another person, allowing one to live vicariously with the person on the screen.[7] It "takes your mind off yourself," so to speak;[8] it operates like a babysitter;[9] and the day and week can be organized around favorite programs.[10] The theme of all of these reasons for viewing television is vicarious living, a reason that one would usually lament in anyone, and perhaps especially so in the elderly, who may be seen to have limited options in life. Because part of the stereotype of the elderly is that they are alone and lonely, it is understandable that research would have looked at how they might compensate for the lacks in their lives. (Snow says that old people are depicted as "asexual eccentrics.")[11] But is this the real reason for television's popularity among elders?

Certainly it is one reason, but there are other, equally salient explanations. An elderly person usually grows more sedentary than he or she was in earlier days. Television is certainly a sedentary pastime, making it a good choice for an individual who is not as active as before. An elderly person, usually retired, also has more leisure time in which to watch TV. The number of hours that he or she has the *potential* of watching is, therefore, greater, and so one would need to take this into account when comparing older viewers with younger ones. And, finally, it is true that the typical elderly person has fewer ties to the world than was true earlier in his or her life. This does not necessarily mean that one is "alone and lonely," as the stereotype suggests, but that the normal workaday world and raising of children are over, meaning that fewer contacts are necessary in day-to-day life. These reasons, spotlighted by Meyersohn in 1961 and cited by Davis,[12] are still relevant today.

There are, however, good outcomes from watching television as well. Television at its best can be life-enhancing, by keeping one interested and well informed in the affairs of the day. Topics of conversation may be gleaned from the daily viewing fare. It is a way to explore the world from an armchair, and this fact makes it a good choice for at least some of the waking hours, perhaps particularly for the elderly. As an aside, it should be noted that in all research on viewing habits, self-reporting of how many hours are watched is likely to be underestimated. People simply do not recall how much television time fills their day. In looking at the research, one must realize that TV is likely to be even more significant than it is usually given credit for.

In the final analysis, it is true that television may serve a compensatory function in the lives of the elderly. What we need to look at, though, is not the damaging effects of too much television, but rather the larger question of how that television viewing fits into a life with normal interactions. The elderly may truly not have as many options open to them as their younger counterparts. If television fills a need in this scenario, perhaps we should look to ways of improving the fare to which one is subjected. The potential exists for television to be a better and more potent force in the lives of the elderly. In many ways, it is unsurpassed as a tool of imparting information. More often than other sources, one accepts as true the information that comes via this medium (whether or not this is good is another question). Given these facts, we can use television to reach elders with vital knowledge of benefits and services available to them. In a more sensitive world, we can develop new images of elders in television programs, helping to form a better, more positive stereotype (in that forming stereotypes is unavoidable). And we can use this new stereotype, along with the information imparted, to influence attitudes toward elders across the age spectrum. Snow points out that television is influential because "people voluntarily (although it seems unconsciously) adopt the perspectives, images . . . employed by television."[13] Certainly this fact can be used to a greater advantage than is now the case in television programming.

## Radio

Radio is often taken for granted. Certainly the people who tune in absentmindedly to start their day are deriving benefit from a medium that they usually do not analyze. Interestingly, though, social scientists have not studied this medium nearly as much as other forms, particularly television. Yet many people in day-to-day life rely on radio far more than they realize to put them in touch with the outer world, whether or not they are active in this outer world. And if their lives are normally outer-directed, people may be prone to listen to radio when alone in order to stimulate companionship. Radio is a medium with potential power to our lives that is usually not recognized.

Radio should also be given credit for its influence on society during the early years of its acceptability by the public—the thirties and forties. (As Snow indicates, it dates its existence to the turn of the century, but it did not "catch on" until much later.) Radio was entertainment in a way somewhat similar to television today; indeed, it was at this time that the prototypes of TV's situation comedies, dramas, and soap operas were developed. While this first role has ceased, the truth is that radio is more popular now than at any other time in its history. There are an average of five radio sets per home, a fact that makes the advertising market quite profitable. Because, as we have noted, people are likely to listen when they are alone, the stations can specialize, presenting programming that appeals to every age segment and interest. In this way, radio functions much as periodicals do, with individuals choosing a station (or magazine) based on their particular subcultures. Snow notes that it is not uncommon for a large city to have thirty or more stations appealing to every conceivable group. And these various groups develop loyalty to their favorite stations; bumper stickers and T-shirts are common items that advertize the listening habits of their wearers.

Unlike the thirties and forties, when programming was more diverse and voice-oriented, the staple of radio programming today is music. The disc jockeys who spin the tunes develop, in their own unique ways, on-the-air personalities that serve, in many cases, for recognizability and popularity. If we can believe their own words to that effect, annnouncers seek to empathize with their audience to a great extent. They visualize their audience in the various activities appropriate to a given time period, and they adjust their mood and verbal commentary accordingly. The pattern of music played can be quite rigid; the air time is segmented, and a specific pattern of tunes is logged and played. A typical pattern is a current hit, followed by a recent hit, a golden oldie, a newcomer, etc. Broadcasters use several strategies to gain the trust of their listeners: an expression of sincerity, a spontaneous and relaxed delivery, and an avoidance of talking down to the listeners. The first two of these can be debatable. Anyone listening to the spiel of an announcer may likely question if sincerity is really achieved; the usual chatter about having a good day can sound trite easily enough. Likewise, it takes real skill to deliver prepared material as though it were spontaneous. But perhaps announcers do achieve this more readily than the obvious presence of sincerity. The third strategy, not talking down to the audience, is based on practical matters; one is not likely to sell as many products if one is being condescending to the listener. Moreover, the announcer's desire to be viewed as a friend enters in; one does not establish superiority over a friend.

As we have noted, radio's influence is much broader than is readily recognized. It is not simply background music or as a source of information (particularly news); it is woven into the fabric of living. Many people, for example, find it disconcerting to drive without having the radio on. The backdrop of music frequently serves to lessen tension. In a survey by Snow of urban listeners from their late teens to middle age, 96 percent said that radio enabled them to relax or to reduce tension; 74 percent claimed that they used radio to obtain or to enhance particular moods.[14] In the latter case, for example, the energetic sounds of Michael Jackson may enliven the audience; rather than using the music to relax, a man or woman may turn on the latest sounds of the current day as motivation to do some disliked chore.

Listening, as we have noted, may substitute for face-to-face companionship. This use is particularly noteworthy, unfortunately, in regard to the aging. Many studies have found that elders frequently feel left out of the mainstream; they are not happy that their children and perhaps others do not turn to them as much as formerly. To fill the gap, they may substitute the media; and radio is well known, in any case, as a companion when one is alone. Elderly people are sometimes alone against their will, and listening to the radio may serve to lessen their loneliness. A general survey of talk shows (not specifically of the elderly) found that people who phone talk-show hosts are generally lonely; 75 percent were single, divorced, or widowed.[15] Other characteristics discovered in this survey were that the individuals calling in desired interpersonal contact more than controversy, belonged to few organizations, and, perhaps surprisingly, were higher than average in educational background.

The individual's link to a given subculture is an important component to radio listening. Most people listen to the same station (or a very limited number of stations) all day, a station that reinforces their life-style. This characteristic serves to promote subculture identity, reinforcing the individual's place in society. In the social scientist's perspective, this means that the individual will derive a sense of belonging by listening to a given station. The radio announcer can even become, for any given person, a significant other who reinforces his or her mutual involvement in a given subculture. Radio thus functions as a reference group. Since almost all radio currently is "live," the listener is involving himself or herself with a very *personal* medium. A particularly apt quotation was made by one talk-show host, who characterized himself as "a social worker in mass communication."[16]

Part of radio's appeal is that it can engage the imagination, creating for the listener a world in which he or she can feel comfortable. Sometimes the lack of visual orientation encourages people to discount the medium, but in actuality the "hearing alone" aspect is a large part of radio's appeal. In the absence of direct visual cues, a listener creates images and elaborates on those described by announcers. This serves to link the listeners to a world, partly of their own making, which appears relevant to their own concerns.

Because radio is a decentralized medium, the many stations in a given area serve to enhance the individuality of the person as well as the multiplicity of cultures in the world. To a great extent, therefore, cultural diversity is enhanced through this medium. This contribution to our way of life may, in fact, be radio's greatest achievement.

## Motion Pictures

Motion pictures have been a part of the society of most of the people who are now older adults. The early years of this new medium were built upon the highly popular vaudeville stage. Here was a medium that promised to entertain, a medium that was pure fun. And Americans went in great numbers to movie houses to take advantage of this new form of entertainment. Snow paints a vivid picture.[17]

In the early years of the century, growth was extremely rapid in the new industry: less than ten years after the first feature film (*The Great Train Robbery*), there were 13,000 motion-picture theaters in the United States.[18] Soon a few film producers acted to form a kind of monopoly, in which theaters were contracted to show only the films of their parent company. Popularity of movies continued to rise through the 1940s (the heyday of the motion picture), and reached a plateau and then a decline only with the advent of television. By the 1960s, movie producers were trying hard to keep their audience (now mostly teenagers and young adults), and frequently failing. Spectaculars often did not live up to their expectations, and eventually with *The Graduate* (1967), producers tried a new formula: a story theme and director could be the stars. Independent film companies came on the scene, and low-budget movies sometimes became major hits. Nevertheless, the lure of the spectacular was still there, and Hollywood produced (and continues to produce) many of these, some with much more success than others (e.g., *Jurassic Park* (1993) and *Indiana Jones and the Temple of Doom* (1984) were major money-makers).

Throughout all of these years, the emphasis in film has been upon basic moral dilemmas and human struggles. Indeed, viewed in this light, movies are a major vehicle for societal catharsis. The main characters struggle with a choice between right and wrong, and individuals are seen to find happiness or tragedy in the process; sex, action, and violence are used at various junctures to enhance interest in the characters' dilemma. Let us take a look at the major categories.

Westerns are a classic favorite of the American people. Moviegoers harken back to a simpler time, when good and evil were less ambiguous and the good guy always won in the end. There is a great deal of idealization in the typical western. The era of cowboys and Indians, although very short in American history (30 years or so), has an appeal that seemingly does not die, in part because of what this era epitomizes about the American spirit. John Wayne best captured this image, and actors in the generations since his great dominance of this type of film have sought to copy the spirit and essence of his portrayal of the great American hero. The western is characterized by a simple plot, heavy stereotypical characters without a great deal of dimension, and plots that vary little from one to the other. The western appeals far more to the emotions than to the intellect, and it is because of this fact that the potential catharsis is so powerful.

Snow's characterization of movies continues with an analysis of the detective story, a form that appeals more to the intellect, combining a complicated "whodunit" plot with a masterful hero who uncovers the evil deeds of the antagonist. In many ways, it is the urban equivalent to the western. Like the western hero, the detective is resourceful, shrewd, smarter than his opponents, and courageous. Perhaps surprisingly, the gangster of both the western and the detective show shares much with the hero of both types of film. Had the bad breaks of life been different, we are led to believe, the bad guy would have turned out all right after all; while not actually inclined to think well of him, we can identify with him to some extent, making him more believable. (The bad "guy" is usually just that—a man.) Moviegoers enjoy a vicarious involvement with his troubles, but rejoice when he falls in the end.

Adventure-thriller movies are made for the joy of the chase, not for character portrayal. Snow characterizes these as having a superhuman hero who demonstrates great physical prowess and pulls off an impossible mission. The audience is attracted by the action almost exclusively. Examples include the familiar James Bond and Superman characters.

Musicals are much revered by the public, particularly when times are tough and society needs a lift. Usually the portrayal is a rags-to-riches story of success, and, along the way, the main characters find love as well. The songs keep the movie going, and plot is all but nonexistent.

The horror movie is a genre that captivates young viewers but is usually not to the taste of older Americans. In horror stories that are done well, suggestion is a large part of the technique. Because shadows and dimly lit views provide much to titillate the imagination, horror films are well suited to a darkened theater. In essence, the films are playing upon the subconscious terrors that all of us have, and as a result these movies can be particularly captivating.

The categories of westerns, detective stories, adventure-thriller movies, musicals, and horror films do not by any means exhaust the genres that are available. Others are love stories, message and morality films on specific social issues, fantasies, films about films, and esoteric products from subcultures and other countries. The types of films have varied little over the years, but the amount of money devoted to various projects has varied tremendously, leading to a boom-or-bust mentality in regard to specific releases. But what does all of this have to do with one's daily life?

It is Snow's thesis that movies may create an experience for the viewer that is every bit as meaningful and significant as other experiences in one's life. He asks, "Can the lingering fear of taking a shower or swimming at night be explained without reference to *Psycho* or *Jaws?*"

Individuals may determine the "right" emotional response from observing the emotional reactions of characters on the screen. It is often true that people get their views of romantic relationships from what they have viewed on the screen. That the sentimentalized view that the screen projects is not realistic may escape the viewer. It is unfortunate that something so vital as our personal relationships can be adversely affected by what we believe "ought" to be true—something that we have learned from going to the movies.

In the same way, as we suggested in regard to westerns and detective stories, people learn what a hero is like from seeing the movies. The movie hero supports certain ideals and values that the viewer incorporates into his or her own value system. People learn both what is acceptable and what is not. Cowboys and Indians do not cry, and it is all right for a soldier to be afraid but not to be a coward. In addition, standards of life-style and fashion are formed and reinforced by motion pictures. It is clear, therefore, that the influence of movies extends far beyond the darkened theater.

The technology that made motion pictures possible, therefore, has altered our society in not only profound ways that we may recognize, but also in quite subtle ways that usually escape attention. The highly visual experience of the motion picture provides images that resonate with some of our deepest feelings, feelings that at the base regulate our interactions with other people. One would be hard-pressed to delineate all the ways that going to the movies has affected one's life.

## Using the Telephone for Human Contact

Elders are well known for their inclination to use the telephone to keep in contact with significant others in their lives. When children are at a distance, when mobility is impaired, when venturing out is difficult for whatever reason, the elder is likely to resort to the intimacy of a medium that brings another's voice, at least, into the living room. As a point of contact, in good times as well as emergencies, the telephone is a unique medium that serves well a variety of needs.[19]

The most important need fulfilled by telephone contact is the social one. For some aging individuals, many hours are spent on the telephone with friends and family. For various reasons, there may not be as much visiting back and forth as in earlier days, and the older person will resort to a way of keeping in touch that demands little in return. Yet, these "few demands" are deceptive. It is actually quite difficult to communicate well with a medium that evokes intimacy, yet distance, and with only aural cues. The telephone speaker has to fill in with imagination the visual aspects of the interaction. In the analysis of Marshall McLuhan, this means that the telephone is a "cool" medium, requiring a great deal more attention to one aspect—vocal nuance—than other means of communication might require.

A second and equally important need fulfilled by the telephone is the safety feature. Family members "check in" on a daily basis, in many cases, to see that everything is going well, and that the older individual has all that he or she needs at the moment. In our highly structured world, where men and women usually work outside the home, and hours are tightly scheduled, this becomes the only way that frequent contact can be made with an aging family member who lives apart. Not only are family or close friends helpful in this regard, but also the elderly person is linked to emergency services. Help is as near as dialing "911" on the phone. In addition, there are agencies that call elders on a regular basis to see that all is well; signals may even be set up in which the elder just answers the phone but does not even talk with the person who is checking to see that everything is all right.

A third important use of the phone is to request services. Today, some former services (such as home delivery of groceries) are no longer available by phone, but others (such as support from social services agencies) are more available than in earlier years. Just by dialing the phone, therefore, one can have access to people and places far beyond one's home. Reaching the correct agency for service could be actually almost impossible if the individual had to walk the streets, but one can make a variety of contacts with ease over the phone, almost without regard to how many further referrals are made.

The telephone is, as we have noted, both intimate and distancing. Callers who are not making private calls have an added sense of talking to one over the phone in an intimate fashion, but of knowing that someone else in the room may be listening. This can be a bit unnerving. The idea itself can be compared with Erving Goffman's description of interaction as having both a "front region" (that is, an intentionally and carefully monitored presentation of ourselves to others), and a "back region" (in which we can relax from our front region performance).[20] Everyone has experienced this sense of duality when conversing over the phone.

Conventions are important in the etiquette of telephone conversation. A careful "dance" is often in effect. One thing that we expect when we call is that we will get the number that we expected. One is always surprised when he or she has dialed a wrong number. The person on the other end, to be polite, only suggests that the number may be wrong: "I think that you have a wrong number." We then apologize, the apology is dismissed, and we hang up—to try again. The whole transaction takes only a few seconds, but in our society it is carefully encoded. If the caller just hangs up upon realizing that he or she has gotten a wrong number, the receiver of the call is likely to feel quite uneasy. The infrequent obscene telephone calls do come to mind.

In conclusion, therefore, we can see that the telephone assists in social interaction and in knitting families and friends together, in some ways bound by convention. It allows one to shop for services within the privacy of one's home. And it is a reassuring medium, being there in the chance of an emergency.

## Computer Technology

This author has queried both specialists in aging and the aging themselves on the likelihood of using computers to answer information needs of the elderly. In the early and mid-eighties, the question was viewed negatively by both groups.[21] It is likely that there has been some more positive orientation since that time, simply because computers have become even more pervasive in our society. It is a commonplace idea, though, that many individuals, including the elderly, who did not "grow up" with computers are slow to take to this technology. This may go so far as an actual distaste on the part of many. It is likely, therefore, that use of the computer in informational transfer for the elderly will lag far behind other segments of the population.

Any shopping list of current and future uses of the computer include aspects of computerization that the elderly could benefit from. This includes everything from shopping by computer (hooked up to the television, perhaps) to using voice mail on the telephone to accessing audiotapes at the local library. A major development is occurring in some areas, in which databases of social-support services are available via computer in the public library. Peoria, Illinois, is one such pioneering site. Certainly the hierarchy of aging services in this country could benefit from a wider knowledge among the elderly of the services that are in fact available to them.

Despite the pervasiveness of computers in our society, few retired elders would need word processing skills, since they are of more use in an office setting. Just as the rest of society benefits from the computerization of goods and services, so too will the elderly. Often, like everybody else, they will be oblivious to the real role of computers in their lives. Few stop to realize that computers are employed to record one more detail of their lives every time a credit card is used. No one, elders included, can escape the ever-present role of computer technology in the modern world.

## Summary

We have traveled through the subject of how we transfer information by first surveying the theory from a social science perspective (chapter 5), then weaving a path through the means for transmission of information—books, periodicals, newspapers, television, radio, motion pictures, telephone, and, finally, computer technology (chapter 6).

It might be appropriate to return to a thought developed earlier: all problems can be viewed on some level as an information need. In this chapter we have taken a firsthand look at the means by which informational transfer is made. Certainly if these means are employed systematically, one will be far more likely to find an answer to a given problem. One must only be willing to seek. And, as we have seen, there is no paucity of means by which to seek.

## Notes

1. For a good, recent articulation of these ideas, see Charles Robinson, "Conflicting Roles of the Public Library," in *Issues for the New Decade: Today's Challenge, Tomorrow's Opportunity*, ed. Alphonse F. Trezza (Boston, Mass.: G. K. Hall, 1991), 81–99.
2. Robert P. Snow, *Creating Media Culture* (Beverly Hills, Calif.: Sage, 1983), 33.
3. Fergus M. Bordewich, "Supermarketing the Newspaper," *Columbia Journalism Review* 16 (September/October 1977): 25.
4. Richard H. Davis, "Television Communication and the Elderly," in *Aging: Scientific Perspectives and Social Issues*, ed. Diana S. Woodruff and James E. Birren (New York: Van Nostrand, 1975), 323.
5. Sebastian De Grazia, "The Uses of Time," in *Aging and Leisure*, ed. Robert Watson Kleemeier (New York: Oxford University Press, 1961), 120.
6. Davis, "Television Communication and the Elderly," 326.
7. Rolf Meyersohn, "A Critical Examination of Commercial Entertainment," in *Aging and Leisure*, ed. Kleemeier, 270.
8. Ira O. Glick and Signey J. Levy, *Living with Television* (Chicago: Aldine, 1962), 55.
9. Ibid., 67.

10. Meyersohn, "Critical Examination," 270, and Glick and Levy, *Living with Television*, 55.
11. Snow, *Creating Media Culture*, 157.
12. Davis, "Television Communication and the Elderly," 326.
13. Snow, *Creating Media Culture*, 147.
14. Ibid., 113.
15. Ibid., 116.
16. Ibid., 120.
17. Ibid., 169–72.
18. Ibid., 201.
19. Garry Mitchell, "Some Aspects of Telephone Socialization," in *Studies in Mass Communication and Technology*, ed. Sari Thomas (Norwood, N.J.: Ablex, 1984): 249–52.
20. Erving Goffman, *Behavior in Public Places* (New York: Free Press, 1963), 25ff.
21. Celia Hales, "How Should the Information Needs of the Aging Be Met? A Delphi Response," *Gerontologist* 25 (April 1985): 172–76; and Celia Hales, "How Should the Information Needs of the Aging Be Met?" Arlington, Va.: ERIC Document Reproduction Service, ED 294 582, 1988.

CHAPTER

# 7

# Asking in One's Immediate Circle

Let us consider information exchange at its most basic: older adults seeking information from the individuals closest to them—spouse, family, neighbors, friends, and professionals with whom they interact in personal matters (e.g., family doctor, personal lawyer, local clergy). We will take as a working definition that any problem can be, on some level, identified as an informational need because the sharing of information is normally attendant to solving problems. Relationships between an individual and the others that we have identified can be considered *primary* in informational transfer because of proximity to the aging individual as well as the fact that the exchange is usually highly individualistic.

There are numerous ways that the inquiry and resultant exchange of information at the primary level can facilitate the elder's well-being personally as well as in society at large. It is not always easy, though, even in this intimate circle, for elders to be willing to ask for help. If the individuals to whom they turn were cognizant of and willing to employ basic communication techniques well known to the helping professions, the resulting exchange would be far more supportive. Our discussion is designed to facilitate this effort.

This chapter will begin with a theoretical foundation for requesting help. The theory will be followed by a survey of the special characteristics of requesting help from each group indicated above—family, friends and neighbors, and helping professionals. In the last case, we will explore what professional "helpers" should do to facilitate easy interaction. We will find that these "how to's" can be applied in everyday life by virtually anyone interested in helping, regardless of one's relationship to that individual.

## Informational Transfer: A Theoretical Foundation

Information is the vital distinguishing element in communication itself; without the exchange of information, there would be almost by definition virtually no communication. By the same token, most problems can be viewed on one level as information needs; i.e., given the right kind of information (one might read "insight"), the problem is much more likely to be resolved. Given these twin concepts—that information forms the basis of communication and that problems are, at base, information needs—we can move easily to the obvious suggestion that an older adult can live more successfully by seeking answers to questions (i.e., seeking information) by communicating with others. Any bit of information, therefore, that reduces the uncertainty of a situation has the potential to improve problem-solving ability.

Communication can be purely "play," in that the individual is enjoying the social interaction but does not use the information in any vital way. Most day-to-day exchanges fit this definition. (An important exception is the fact that one never knows when a chance remark will have major applicability to another's life.) But when individuals have what is termed a "serious conversation," they are typically seeking real answers to real problems. In social science terms, this means that they are seeking from communication the wherewithal to structure or organize their environment so that they can choose the right action in a given situation. They are seeking information that will make their decision easier. They are not necessarily asking what the answer should be, *even when they ask what they should do*. Many misunderstandings arise at this point. An individual asks advice, and then, when that advice is not taken, the individual from whom advice had been sought takes offense.

The best analysis of family-and-friend interaction that appears in the literature is given by Lois M. Tamir.[1] Her analysis makes clear that the commonplace happening of normal interaction makes more sense in a greater context. The fact that most people, elders included, do not like asking for help is a given addressed in all of its ramifications by Bengtson and Cutler.[2] A simple request for help may be quite threatening to the requester. This is especially true for elders, who are more prone, perhaps, than younger people to fear that they are losing control and cannot manage life as well as they once did. Elders can also fear the exchange on an unconscious level because it may signal a loss of power in the relationship.[3] The perception is that the weak or infirm ask for help, and, by extension, perhaps the elderly as well—implying all the while that they are ill or infirm.

At its best, asking will be a two-way exchange, in which information is given and received, and then is brought to bear on the problem. If it is seen to be a one-way exchange, in which one seeks help and receives that assistance, the attitude of the elder may be particularly negative about the exchange. As we implied earlier, few people like to be told what to do, *even when they ask*. People, elders included, like to feel that they are still in control and managing their own affairs. Any condescension on the part of others will be keenly noted and, probably, resented. In the best type of exchange, the solution to a given problem may be discussed openly and as equals, leaving the elder to determine (perhaps later, after the conversation ends) if the solution is useful.

Face-to-face communication involves all the senses; theoretically, therefore, it should be superior to other forms, such as telephoning, for example, in which only hearing is used. When several senses are being activated, though, one must weigh the benefits of this versus the fact that concentration could be focused on only one sense, as in the telephone. And there is a possibility of overwhelming the person with too much sensory input, thereby being "tuned out." In the absence of illness, though, it is generally possible for not only more information but more complete information to be imparted in a face-to-face environment.

A high percentage of the information that is given face-to-face is imparted inadvertently and is nonverbal. And, of course, unlike technological means, there is no permanent storage (other than memory) to which one can refer later. Ultimately, the key to successful communication is the ability of the participants to grasp the information implicit within the conversation. The communication that results can be instrumental in assisting an individual to maintain the status quo—his or her normal level of functioning in society. In times of crisis, however, the communication is more urgent. It becomes a matter of attempting to confront successfully the more problematic issues of life and facing down the worst consequences.

Tamir discusses the context in which conversation is meaningful; for example, just the inquiry, "How's it going?" is meaningless without knowing the relationship of speaker to listener, their knowledge of each other's lives, the context in which the words are spoken.[4] Tamir lists four basic components to understanding dialogue: (1) shared background, (2) shared rules and norms for interpersonal behavior, (3) the capacity to take the role of the other, and (4) consensus about the relationship between the interacting individuals. We will discuss each in turn.

First, let's consider shared background. Tamir relates an anecdotal example that is especially cogent.[5] If John says to Mary, "Chicken is on sale today," and Mary's face lights up, it is because more information than this simple statement has been transmitted. Do John and Mary both especially like chicken? And have chickens been higher than normal lately? Are they going to go out and take advantage of a bargain immediately? Is it likely that they will have chicken for dinner tonight? Any and all of these contextual meanings may be implied in the initial statement, for which we would have to know Mary and John and their lives together. In fact, the closer two individuals are, the less need be said because shared background is so great.

Many husbands and wives speak a kind of "shorthand" to each other, in which each is intimately understood by the other, but from which an outsider would be completely excluded. Intensive relationships in particular are noted for their shared background, making communication not only more intense but also more enjoyable. The thread of knowledge is carried along by tenuous words and indirect references that others would miss entirely.

Second, Tamir suggests that individuals in conversation are likely to share certain rules and norms for everyday conduct. The term "speech community" has been coined to denote the individuals for whom social behavior is similar and who therefore share various norms for conduct. The use of code words is an example of speaking that has a meaning beyond the words themselves and which suggests a shared social environment.

Third, Tamir says that the ability to take the role of another is fundamental to successful communication. Children develop this skill early in life, with the ones who are most successful frequently becoming the most popular. The ability to understand the perspective of the other has widespread implications for success in life, both work and play.

The fourth component of successful communication, as outlined by Tamir, is the recognition of the relationship between speaker and listener. As in our example of Mary and John and the chickens on sale, it is even possible that John is speaking after a disagreement, and that he is seeking to make the peace via an exchange that will be satisfying to both of them. One cannot understand a statement without knowing something about the relationship of the two people involved.

Much that passes between two people is nonverbal, as we have noted. For example, dialogue that is smooth and unstressed is characterized by similar pauses in the dialogue; stress changes the cadences. Other nonverbal behavior, such as body movement, posture, gaze, etc., has been correlated with the range and depth of emotional feeling between the speakers. The more similar individuals perceive themselves to be, and the greater liking between the individuals, the more similarity exists in these nonverbal behaviors.

Let us turn now to each of the primary groups.

## Information Transfer within the Family

The family influences a given individual more than any other social group; this is so obvious as to be overlooked in many assessments of need. No other relationships are so intense nor so enduring—whether we speak of the immediate family of the child, the adult family of which he or she is a parent, or the elder's family, which may consist of several generations of offspring.

The vast majority of older adults live independently in their own households with a spouse. The most important source of information within intimate circles is usually, therefore, the marriage partner. As we have seen in chapters 3 and 4, marriage is clearly an important focus in the older years, perhaps as much as (if not more than) during the honeymoon period, and we can see now that the informational aspect is merely one part of the entire interdependent framework. As Tamir indicates, once the children have left home, husband and wife are more free to dedicate their time and energy to one another.[6]

In a good marriage, commitment and companionship have typically risen in importance over the years, ensuring that the older adult is likely to see his or her spouse as the most important person to consult about day-to-day problems. Whether or not this choice is wise differs among people for any number of reasons. One of the common problems for older adults is that their horizons have shrunk, making them less able to "keep up" with society's changes and, along with this, less able to obtain the information they need to function successfully. Because a spouse is likely to share many characteristics with his or her partner, the partner is sometimes just as likely (or unlikely) to have the answer as the spouse. Neither is probably working outside the home, for example, which closes off the network of business/vocational acquaintances who might have the answer to a given problem. On the other hand, the spouse knows his or her partner as no other does, and this intimate knowledge can be a blessing. We turn to our closest relationships to help us solve problems because we trust them to have our best interests at heart; this "heart" knowledge ensures that the communication will be understood on nonverbal as well as verbal levels. Because we are known so deeply and well, we frequently take the advice that they give us over any advice, however well intentioned or good, by a stranger. This influence is so great that we would be well advised to use caution in seeking to solve the problems of our nearest and dearest. As Tamir says, "Few relationships of later life can convey the sense of self-confirmation derived from the mutuality and self-understanding when husband and wife communicate."[7]

When looking at the family beyond just the spouse, we find the potential for influence to be great. Historically, societies that put a great premium on the knowledge and expertise of the elderly were particularly revering of the older generation. In our society, however, great change has rendered much knowledge of the aging to be obsolete, and this has led to a subtle (or even overt) discrimination toward the older adult. The continued support of the older adult by others in the family, particularly his or her children and grandchildren, can go a long way toward counteracting the negative effects of society's view.

Tamir relates that the family's influence has been found to be important in a number of ways: in directing participation in societal institutions;[8] in influencing behavior both inside the family and outside in society;[9] and in developing consensus about how to interpret the world.[10] All of these research findings have relevance that can be equated with informational transfer, keeping in mind our thesis that any problem can on some level be viewed as an information need.

In the first instance—participation in societal institutions—the individual may not seek help in the larger society if the family is opposed. A common example might be a need on the part of one family member for psychological counseling. Unless there is support for acknowledging this need and seeking an answer through professionals, the individual may struggle alone with the problem. This decision, in turn, may be very detrimental to the functioning of the family itself. Because of society's historical stigma and resistance to such help, older adults may be particularly influenced by the family's reaction in such an example.

In the second instance—behavior both within and outside the family—influence of the family is so deep-seated that its pervasive influence may go unrecognized for what it is. Children acquire many of their beliefs from their family, and then spend their adolescent years in rebellion from at least some of them, only to reencounter echoes of their parents in deeds that are "just like her mother" (or "just like his father"). The family bonds and training that a child has received are nearly impossible to discard. In our informational context, if studying books to get answers to questions is a habit in the family, then this behavior is likely to be replicated by various family members. If a lifelong habit is formed, older adults are likely to continue the pattern.

Finally, as one develops ways in which to view the world, the family is pivotal. If a college education is seen as an important factor in succeeding as an adult, most family members will seek one, and this pattern will continue beyond one generation. Because higher education is less common among older adults, the aging themselves may not have the college degree, but their own attitude and perhaps disappointment in not acquiring this credential for themselves may influence whether or not their children (as well as their grandchildren) will seek the degree.

Tamir concludes that Sussman, Sussman and Burchinal, Troll, and Troll and Smith have all stipulated that most families can be classified as "modified extended."[11] By definition, this refers to a network of several related nuclear units, usually living within visiting distance. This network is advantageous in our highly urban and impersonal society; contrary to myth, this network does commonly support its elderly members. The help may be in the form of mutual aid or social interaction, as well as the important tie of love and companionship. Although mere proximity to another does not ensure a satisfactory relationship, one statistic that is particularly reassuring to older people is the fact that about 90 percent of the older people in the United States with living children live less than an hour's trip from at least one of those children. Of those with living children, 55 percent had seen at least one of them within the past day or so and another 26 percent had seen one of their children in the past week.[12] But the aid is not always flowing equally toward or away from the elders; no one generation comes off clearly as a giver or receiver in the research studies.[13] Let us make a closer examination of the interdependence of the modified extended family.

Research studies conflict in the matter of interdependence. Some have found that the proportion of elders who gave help to their children is greater than the proportion who received, but others have found just the reverse.[14] A study of the social classes of the respondents indicates a possible reason for the difference: middle-class adult children are more likely to receive help from their parents, whereas in the working class, elders are more likely to receive support, financial and otherwise. A large study by Hill determined that grandparents received much more than they gave in terms of emotional gratification, household management, and illness support, but in economic support, grandparents gave almost as much as they received.[15] Grandparents do underreport their own contributions, however.[16] Hill's study was skewed toward the working class, and so it is debatable how precise the figures would be for the middle and upper classes.

Some studies have found that aging individuals who report satisfactory relationships with their adult children may form friendships with other people more readily than those who report poor relationships within the family.[17] The reasons for this finding are not reported, but it is possible that a "gift" for relationships has here been uncovered; it is also possible that a child is fulfilling emotional needs for the parent, who then feels more eager to reach out to others. Certainly the person who is rich in relationships—of friends or family—is more likely to have his or her informational, as well as other, needs met. Problems can be more readily solved when the network of individuals who can help is quite wide. If one individual does not have the answer that is needed, it is possible that yet another one will. Moreover, if an elder is temperamentally willing to reach out to others in time of need, there is a much healthier prognosis; suffering in silence and alone is not likely to produce a positive outcome.

One element of significant importance in resolving problems is the degree to which families assist when bureaucratic institutions have to be brought in. Usually the adult child, contrary to myth, supports his or her parent(s) in caring ways that go far beyond obligation or duty, and that may even become debilitating to himself or herself, before professional help is sought. Once professional help enters the picture, moreover, the adult child remains very involved. The evidence points to considerable influence in decision-making vis-à-vis the older person's relationship with the institution. Families are frequently buffers in the elder's dealings with the institution; they examine the service options, monitor the contact, and assess what changes need to be made as time passes.[18] The need of an elderly person may be, in fact, the need of a family; unfortunately, however, our bureaucratic institutions are not organized to see need in just this way.

We know that the role reversal implied in the previous paragraph is not easily accomplished. The happiest interaction between adult children and their parents is when both are functioning well. Neither increasing dependence of the elder nor continuing nurturance of the adult child is a happy solution.[19] Part of the difficulty is the differences in values between generations. Atchley suggests that differences in drinking practices, childbearing attitudes, manners and etiquette, and religious beliefs are all major obstacles to good communication between the generations.[20] Another obstacle is the adult child's reluctance to take advice, often accompanied by a strong need on the part of the older parent to give advice. Elders were found, in one study, to believe that it was their right and duty to advise their grown children.[21]

It is unlikely that most parent-child relationships escape a power struggle of some sort. When the child is young, he or she depends on the parent. When that child become an adult, he or she becomes accustomed to handling his or her own problems, independent of the parent (despite the parent's tendency to advise, discussed above). And when the parent becomes very old or in ill health, it is quite likely that the dependence will be reversed; the adult child becomes "parent" to the parent. This role reversal does not come easily to either generation.

By contrast, Blenkner has suggested a better model for both generations to follow: that of "filial maturity."[22] This model suggests that a middle-aged adult will identify with the parent in a deeper and richer way, because the adult child with maturity will view his or her parent from a wider perspective. This model implies also that the adult child will be sensitive to the difficulties inherent in assuming greater responsibility for the parent as he or she ages. The possibility of greater dependency, and the actuality of greater dependency, is typically a profoundly threatening prospect for the older adult.

If power struggles, such as they are, are reflections of unresolved problems in the parent-child relationship from earlier years, the prognosis is less positive than if the difficulty does not have these deep-seated roots. If the parent and child have enjoyed a good relationship over the years, then the problems in role reversal or the need for "filial maturity" will be lessened.

Given these problems of shifting power, dependency, etc., we might wonder about the extent to which the older generation is alienated. Individuals in institutions that work with the elderly report much higher levels of alienation between parents and children than research studies uncover. The reason is obvious: institutional help comes, frequently, when children have failed to provide. The older people that professionals see are disproportionately alienated and neglected; otherwise there would be less reason for them to seek professional help. But when the entire population is considered, the situation is as Blenkner reported: "The older adult prefers to maintain his independence as long as he can, but . . . when he can no longer manage for himself, he expects his children to assume that responsibility; his children in turn expect to, and do, undertake it, particularly in terms of personal and projective services."[23]

The roles of spouse and parent or child come typically to mind when one is considering significant others, but the fact is that the role of sibling is the most common for elders.[24] Although having a spouse is the best predictor for successful adjustment to elderly living, having one or more siblings who are close and attentive may be the next best option. Unlike parent-child relationships, in a relationship between siblings, the power is usually shared.[25] Interaction may, as a result, be more comfortable. Of course, since individuals come from the same generation, the likelihood of solving problems by getting information from a sister or brother is akin to the likelihood of receiving help from a spouse. Because of long years of love and companionship, which may have been strengthened in the later years, the nonverbal communication is likely to be especially keen, and all the advantages for this are present in interaction between siblings.

## Seeking Information from Friends and Neighbors

Friends and neighbors are certainly not synonymous terms, but it is frequently true that proximity breeds friendship. Much in the older adult's informational world is dependent upon where he or she lives and with whom he or she is in close quarters. Because of the ease with which research studies can be done in that setting, often senior dwelling complexes are the focus for studies that analyze proximity and neighborliness among elders. Dwellings may range from low-income public housing to expensive retirement communities. It should be noted, however, that although retirement group residents have been studied frequently, only a small proportion of the elderly actually live in this setting. The degree to which the studies can predict for the whole is thus an open question. We will reluctantly, however, make the assumption (which has been made by most sociologists as well) that the findings can generally be applied to other settings.

Tamir makes the point that the elderly move far less often than younger people.[26] There are strong forces to cause the elderly to "age in place," and it is often only a crisis situation that will prompt a move. Most elders report satisfaction with their environment. One primary reason is the network of friendships that one is likely to have in the neighborhood.[27] This is a prime setting for informational transfer. In a traditional neighborhood, the relationships have been formed over a long period, making for trust and familiarity. In addition, there is little or no hint of the power struggle that elders sometimes encounter with their adult children. Asking friends for help in solving problems does not carry the threat or the negative emotional overtones that the same request does when made of one's own blood kin. Leaning over the back fence to casually request a bit of information that one needs, but hesitates to ask for, is a familiar and comfortable—as well as nonthreatening—situation. In addition, given patterns of "aging in place," it is likely that the neighbor to whom one turns is also an elder. Perhaps the individual will share the same world view, making for enhanced communication. It is even possible that he or she has, due to age, encountered the same problem or knows of someone who has. If we can postulate that similar problems affect cohort generations, it is reassuring to turn to those of similar age, but with somewhat different experiences, for assistance.

If one's environment includes many elders, Tamir notes that it is likely that a given person will have more friends.[28] This is particularly interesting from an informational, communicational viewpoint. The more one reaches out for help, as we have noted above, the greater the likelihood that one will find needed answers. It is also likely, by this same reasoning, that the more friends one has of whom he or she can seek answers, the greater the likelihood of receiving help. This scenario might work only with the proviso that the friendships are relatively close and not generally superficial. Depending upon the content of the question and the personality of the inquirer, one may conceivably not ask for information from a casual acquaintance as readily as from a real friend. On the other hand, however, certain types of threatening questions may be more readily asked in relative anonymity; there is little evidence to suggest that individuals would be willing, though, to seek out relative strangers in order to preserve their anonymity in the asking of a sensitive question. In most cases, the reverse would be true.

Another advantage of a relatively age-segregated environment is that residents are protected from ridicule and from feelings of inadequacy when they are compared with younger adults.[29] Fear of ridicule or rejection is a prime reason that one does not seek help when he or she needs it.

The age-segregated retirement communities that have served as the backdrop for many research studies are tailor-made for social interaction, and thus informational transfer. Communities such as these form their own set of norms and so establish age-appropriate behaviors where there may have been uncertainty before. The older adult is therefore supported by the immediate society of which he or she is a part.[30] And, it is true in context as well as in traditional settings, as we have noted, that the words "neighbor" and "friend" are often synonymous.

A positive development for information transfer is the fact that as people age, their requirements for friendship become less stringent. One is more open to a greater range of people. Research has shown that pre-adults (age nineteen and under) believe that friendship should include a whole host of qualities: acceptance, mutual liking, trust, enjoyment, respect, loyalty, mutual aid, and shared recreation, talk, and ideas. Mature adults need fewer qualities to call a person a friend: respect, mutual liking, enjoyment, trust, and mutual aid. Elderly adults (age seventy and over) need the fewest qualities of all: just acceptance and trust. While it may appear from this that the aging person (throughout life) is becoming less discriminating, a better way to analyze the finding is to believe that people become more tolerant of others' differences as they age. This will ensure that one develops friendships from people of widely differing experiences, and thus the possibility is great that help will be forthcoming on diverse issues because of a greater range of background among friends. The tendency is, nevertheless, to select friends from the same social class, and this is a limiting feature.

Rosow analyzed friendship among the elderly in an in-depth analysis that identified five friendship patterns.[31] First, the "cosmopolitan," a predominantly middle-class group, had the least contact with neighbors and no desire for more friends. They had interests that extended beyond the immediate residential area. Second, the "phlegmatic" (constituting only 4 percent of the sample) had likewise little contact with neighbors and no desire for more friends, but was predominantly working class and was satisfied with little social life outside their children's visits. Third, the "isolated," who had little contact but wanted more, was predominantly middle class but lacked social skills for making friends easily. Fourth, the "sociable" had frequent contact with friends and neighbors and no desire for more friends. This group was primarily working class, female, and widowed. Fifth, the "insatiable" had frequent contact with friends and neighbors, yet desired more. They were primarily gathering acquaintances but their contacts had little depth.

Of these five groupings, only the "isolated" and the "insatiable" are actually problemmatic resolutions to the friendship issue. Isolation will hinder the satisfaction of many needs in old age, and the indiscriminate pseudosharing of the insatiable does not allow for any real communication.

What can be termed "quality friendships" are a prized commodity in today's impersonal world. Insofar as psychological well-being is concerned, having a confidant is one of the surest routes to wellness. We will define a confidant as a friend with whom one shares the deepest thoughts and concerns.[32] This definition implies significant self-disclosure, a prime requirement if one is to get informational needs satisfied in an optimal fashion.

If one has a social life but lacks a confidant, it is better than no social life; but the absence may be keen nevertheless. However, if one lacks a social life as well as a confidant, Tamir notes that the impact of isolation may be devastating, leading in some cases to depression.[33] (The *loss* of a confidant is also likely to lead to depression.) It was found that a confidant relationship serves as a buffer against the social losses that accompany aging. And no one person filling a given role is necessary for confidant status; a spouse, child, or friend is equally likely to serve as a confidant. Perhaps surprisingly, however, elderly men are more likely to name their wives as their confidant than vice versa. This relationship can, in part, account for the tendency of older men to remarry relatively soon after a wife dies; the wife provides the only confidant relationship that the husbands knows and feels that he needs.

In terms of social class, those of the middle class and above are more likely to have a confidant than those of the working class. This finding is similar to the finding that middle-class adults have more friends than working class adults.[34]

Certainly it is understandable that to have a true friend with which one may share the difficult problems as well as joys of life is a strong plus for optimal aging. If one can turn to this confidant in the trials of life, he or she can find renewal and an increased zest for living. The emotional support is crucial. Just as likely is the fact that informational needs will be satisfied first by inquiring of this significant other; if the confidant does not have the answer, perhaps together they can turn to someone who does. Whatever the case, the inquirer knows that the confidant is there, willing to help solve whatever problem has arisen.

## Inquiring of Intimate Professionals

We have chosen to term those in the professional world who have the closest ties to the older adult—typically the person's physician, lawyer, or clergyman—an "intimate professional." This suggests that the type of information that will be forthcoming from these people will be of an intimate nature, not only in the classification of the assistance, but also in the depth of the relationship itself. Frequently, the ties are, optimally, longstanding, and therefore the degree of mutual understanding is very great. There is some indication that these bonds are much less binding in our society today than in earlier eras.

In our society, the old familiar ties with professionals that individuals have enjoyed are at risk today. As a result, there has emerged an unfortunate negative bias against some of the professions that used to be held in highest esteem. Lawyers have suffered from negative stereotyping for a number of years, and now, with rising medical costs and the impersonality of a large society, physicians are suffering much the same fate. The clergy may be the only profession central to the "helping professions" to be still held in high regard, and yet there is evidence that few individuals, even among the "faithful," still accord the voice of the clergy the value and authority that their parents did.

What impact does this have upon their usefulness in meeting informational needs? If an elder does not know very well or does not greatly respect one of the professionals to whom he or she would otherwise turn, then the possibility of having one's problems sympathetically resolved is greatly diminished. The professional preparation of the lawyer, physician, or clergy *should* better prepare that person to answer questions, to satisfy informational and other needs, and to resolve problems in his or her given field of expertise. But this professional preparation will not be optimally utilized if the elder who is seeking help hesitates to do so when that is in fact the best solution to the difficulty. An elder who is turned off by professionals will turn to less well prepared "helpers," or do without. And as a result, society as a whole will be the lesser for it. One hallmark of a successfully functioning society is the degree to which it is responsive to the needs of its members. If elders and others do not turn to the people who, by education and experience, are best able to answer specific legal, medical, or religious questions, then we have a communicational and informational breakdown.

This is not to suggest that such a breakdown has already occurred, but there are indications that we are at risk. Given this, therefore, what might professionals do on a personal level to increase communication? For an answer, let us turn to the counseling techniques that are advised for these so-called "helping" professions.[35] While not every problem represents a counseling situation, the techniques used in counseling can certainly be applied to the communication of any given problem by a client to a professional, or, as we will call the latter, a "helper."

Studies have found that older adults prefer professionals of their same age range. This can suggest empathy, but it can also suggest a negative feeling felt because of bias or age discrimination. This tendency is particularly strong in the helping professions, unfortunately, and it is keenly perceived by the aging themselves. As helpers listen to the aging, they are assessing the problem, first and foremost, but there are secondary considerations as well. Is the helper truly "open" to the elder, listening carefully but not condescendingly, and without judging him or her? The elder is likely to hesitate to relate the problem anyway, and any evidence of being negatively evaluated will have a devastating impact on the exchange. Sometimes the elder will feel uncomfortable by what he or she hears himself saying, and his sense of strain will transfer into negativity toward the helper. And sometimes the elder will not be able to articulate the problem well, and groping for the right words may make him or her seem nervous or confused. All of this should not matter if the helper is truly meeting the elder at the point of his or her need, which is to say that the helper is "really there" for the elder. This takes great skill, and not even the best communicator is able to establish a good rapport with every individual. But there are certain practical considerations that can be applied to turn around even the most difficult interaction. Most of these considerations serve to heighten the empathy between the elder and helper; in total, they comprise a set of core values for helping.

### *Twin Values*

Egan describes this optimal behavior under two umbrella concepts: respect and genuineness.[36] He says that the entire structure of the helping process rests on these twin values. Neither value is usually communicated in words directly; while the helper may initially indicate respect by his or her choice of words, the sense that respect is actually felt will depend far more on body posture, facial expression, and general manner than on anything that is said. The same is true also for genuineness. How might a helper communicate these values?

**Respect**

Egan describes "being for" the client as the first element in respect. This attitude suggests that the helper recognizes the basic humanity of the client and (if necessary) indicates that the helper acknowledges that clients are able to be "more than they are right now." Helpers should be willing and able to work, to fulfill their part of the contract between helper and client. The client's problem is, in effect, worth the time and energy that it will take to resolve. This involves the recognition that no problem is small or insignificant if it is causing concern for the client; no problem can be seen as trivial if a client has cared enough to seek help. Similarly, no problem is identical to another; each client brings his own unique set of characteristics to whatever issue is under discussion. Consequently, the client uniqueness should be well regarded by the helper. Self-determination on the part of the client is also fundamental. The helper needs to empower the client to solve his or her own problem; although indications of a right course of action are a part of the counseling process, the actual choice of what to do should come from the client. Otherwise, he or she does not "own" the solution. Attendant to this is the fact that the client should be able, next time, to marshal resources to better face an obstacle. If handled in the right way, the client will not see the helper as a panacea, to hand out solutions or say what to do, but rather as a catalyst to assist in the decision-making process. Helpers should assume that the client is willing to carry out his or her part in solving the problem; while lack of motivation on the part of clients can be an issue, it should not be assumed to be present. Nearly always it masks the real issue of self-empowerment, and as such it can become a goal in the counseling process itself. It goes without saying that confidentiality should always be upheld in the counseling process; if there are any indications that confidentiality *cannot* be upheld, the client should be so informed early in the interaction.

We have earlier mentioned body posture as important. An attentive posture connotes interest and will ensure that the client is aware of really being "listened to." Specifics of this, as outlined by Egan, are the following: Face the client squarely. Keep an open posture. Lean toward the client. Maintain good eye contact. And try to remain relaxed. We have also indicated that it is wise to suspend critical judgment; this does not mean that one condones any action, but simply is open to what is being said. If one does in fact condemn, the disclosure will probably be less than complete on the part of the client; most people are quite quick to pick up on negative judgments and to censor their own responses. Akin to this is the necessity to communicate understanding. People generally believe that others respect them if they spend time and effort in trying to understand them. Communicating warmth is also advantageous. Most people respond better to helpers who are responsive and caring people. It is good not to carry this to extremes lest one appear insincere. Genuine warmth takes time to develop in any relationship.

**Genuineness**

Gibb expresses a number of actions that, in summary, show that one should not overemphasize one's role in the helping process.[37] If a helper is overly aware of the professional "hat" he or she wears, there may be a breakdown in real helpfulness. Sometimes this extends to an awareness of how one's credentials are interpreted by clients. Having the "right" degrees and communicating this fact to a client, by word or deed, is likely to be a real turnoff. Simply meeting one another as people usually works best. Certainly the degrees should help; after all, the knowledge base that they represent are the reason that one's help has been sought in the first place. But one can err greatly by wanting to be seen as the "expert." After all, the client is the true expert on the particular problem that he or she brings for solution. Regardless of how similar that problem may be to others like it, the story attendant to it is the client's own and can be told better by no one else.

Egan notes that a degree of spontaneity is advantageous. It will enhance empathy in the helper-client interaction. If the client believes that the helper is reacting to the client with responses that are geared to that problem and that alone, he or she will be favorably disposed to share more. If the helper appears to give stock responses and (probably) reacts as if he or she has heard this all before, the client will share less with the helper, and the real problem will less likely be uncovered.

Helpers need to be assertive without being aggressive. A cardinal problem of many trainees in the helping professions is that they are afraid to assert themselves. Frequently, one has heard much about being "nondirective" and helping the client to formulate his or her own solution, and this tends to inhibit *enough* direction. Clients, after all, have thus far failed to find their own solution and that is why they have come to a professional. Certainly they want to get their money's worth. A helper who actively *points in the direction*, at least, of various solutions will not be guilty of overhelping.

Other characteristics that enhance genuineness in the interaction are nondefensive behavior, consistency, and openness. These traits come with experience more often than not. A helper who trusts his or her own judgment will soon learn that a lack of defensiveness is the *best* defense. Being willing to face possible errors without apologizing for being human is a hard-earned outgrowth of years of professional consulting. The earlier in one's career that one learns it, the better.

Consequently, we see that cultivating respect for the client and adopting an attitude of genuineness toward the client are recommended for all who seek to be helping professionals. These twin values can be seen as a way to comprehend a myriad of positive traits that would enhance the client-helper relationship. We can readily see that even nonprofessionals can adopt some of these same traits to benefit. While no family member or friend should pretend to mimic a professional counselor (and probably would be rejected for so trying), any communication at all could benefit from the positive traits that represent counseling at its best. Moreover, family members and friends help, not because they are paid but rather because they *care;* this fact increases their value to the individual seeking help. How much more benefit might one be if the lay helper adopted the acceptance that is valued in the professional helper? Certainly acceptance as well as other positive traits would serve to open communication channels between *any* two individuals, and therefore increase the likelihood that problems will be resolved.

## Summary

We have provided a theoretical framework for understanding a simple request for help, seen in our context as resolving a problem that is usually, at base, an informational need. And we have looked at some of the characteristics of "asking" behavior by elders toward the individuals who are closest to them. Finally, we have discussed practical ways in which helpers of whatever category can assist a needy individual. In moving from theory to particulars and finally to practicalities, we should never lose sight of the fact mentioned early on: Elders, like most of us, don't like to ask for help. To the extent that asking for information is actually asking for help, the same situation holds. In large part society is responsible for augmenting this natural reluctance in the aging. Because we sometimes discriminate against the elderly, they in turn are less prone to place themselves in a position that accentuates their vulnerability. Nobody likes to advertize their vulnerabilities, but at the same time none of us are always in command and on top of the situations that life throws at us. If we can see an aging person who asks for information (or help) as one who *temporarily* is in need, the exchange will be better. We must affirm their self-worth by not emphasizing weakness, and one way to do this is to realize that the individual is managing well in other areas and will eventually manage well in his or her needy area as well.

## Notes

1. Lois M. Tamir, *Communication and the Aging Process* (New York: Pergamon, 1979).
2. Vern L. Bengtson and Neal E. Cutler, "Generations and Intergenerational Relations," in *Handbook of Aging and the Social Sciences*, ed. Robert H. Binstock and Ethel Shanas (New York: Van Nostrand, 1976), 130–59.
3. Tamir, *Communication and the Aging Process*, 115.
4. Lois M. Tamir, "The Older Person's Communication Needs: The Perspective of Developmental Psychology," in *Communications Technology and the Elderly: Issues and Forecasts*, ed. Ruth E. Dunkle, Marie R. Haugh, and Marvin Rosenberg (New York: Springer, 1984), 28–31.
5. Ibid., 28.
6. See Lillian E. Troll, "The Family in Later Life: A Decade Review," *Journal of Marriage and the Family* 33 (1971): 263–90.
7. Tamir, *Communication and the Aging Process*, 114.
8. William J. Goode, "A Theory of Role Strain," *American Sociological Review* 25 (August 1960): 483–96; and Walter J. Gove et al., "The Family Life Cycle: Internal Dynamics and Social Consequences," *Sociology and Social Research* 57 (January 1973): 182–95.
9. Tamir, *Communication and the Aging Process*, 113; Gove et al., "The Family Life Cycle"; and Marvin B. Sussman and Lee Burchinal, "Kin Family Network: Unheralded Structure in Current Conceptualizations of Family Functioning," *Marriage and Family Living* 24 (August 1962): 231–40.
10. Arthur P. Bochner, Edmund P. Kaminski, and Mary Anne Fitzpatrick, "The Conceptual Domain of Interpersonal Commmunication Behavior: A Factor-Analytic Study," *Human Communication Research* 3 (Summer 1977): 291–302.
11. Marvin B. Sussman, "The Family Life of Old People," in Binstock and Shanas, eds., *Handbook of Aging*, 218–43; Sussman and Burchinal, "Kin Family Network"; Troll, "The Family in Later Life"; and Lillian E. Troll and Jean Smith, "Attach-

ment through the Life Span: Some Questions about Dyadic Bonds among Adults," *Human Development* 19 (1976): 156–70.

12. Adrienne E. Harris, "Social Dialectics and Language: Mother and Child Construct the Discourse," *Human Development* 18 (1975): 80–96.
13. Robert C. Atchley, *Social Forces and Aging*, 4th ed. (Belmont, Calif.: Wadsworth, 1985), 143–44.
14. Gordon F. Streib, "Intergenerational Relations: Perspectives of the Two Generations on the Older Parent," *Journal of Marriage and the Family* 27 (November 1965): 469–76; and Ethel Shanas, "Family Help Patterns and Social Class in Three Countries," *Journal of Marriage and the Family* 29 (May 1967): 257–66.
15. Reuben Hill, "Decision Making and the Family Life Cycle," in *Social Structure and the Family*, ed. Ethel Shanas and Gordon F. Streib (Englewood Cliffs, N.J.: Prentice-Hall, 1965): 113–39.
16. Vern L. Bengtson and Neal E. Cutler, "Generations and Intergenerational Relations: Perspectives on Age Groups and Social Change," in Binstock and Shanas, eds., *Handbook of Aging*, 147.
17. Gary D. Hampe and Audie L. Blevins, Jr., "Primary Group Interaction of Residents in a Retirement Hotel," *International Journal of Aging and Human Development* 6 (1975): 209–20.
18. Ethel Shanas and Marvin B. Sussman, *Family, Bureaucracy, and the Elderly* (Durham, N.C.: Duke University Press, 1977), 216.
19. Margaret Clark and Barbara Gallatin Anderson, *Culture and Aging: Anthropological Study of Older Americans* (Springfield, Ill.: C. C. Thomas, 1967), 275–76.
20. Atchley, *Social Forces and Aging*, 143–44.
21. Joseph H. Britton and Jean O. Britton, "The Middle-Aged and Older Rural Person and His Family," in *Older Rural Americans*, ed. E. Grant Youmans (Lexington: University of Kentucky, 1967): 44–74.
22. Margaret Blenkner, "Social Work and Family Relationships in Later Life with Some Thoughts on Filial Maturity," in Shanas and Streib, eds., *Social Structure and the Family*, 46–59.
23. Ibid., 48.
24. Clark and Anderson, *Culture and Aging*, 294.
25. Marjorie F. Lowenthal and Betsy Robinson, "Social Networks and Isolation," in Binstock and Shanas, eds., *Handbook of Aging*, 432–56; and Troll, "The Family in Later Life," 263–90.
26. See M. Powell Lawton, "The Impact of the Environment on Aging and Behavior," in *Handbook of the Psychology of Aging*, ed. James E. Birren and K. Warner Schaie (New York: Van Nostrand, 1977), 290.
27. Tamir, *Communication and the Aging Process*, 123.
28. See Gordon F. Streib, "Social Stratification and Aging," in Binstock and Shanas, eds., *Handbook of Aging*, 171–72.
29. Frances M. Carp, "Housing and Living Environment of Older People," in Binstock and Shanas, eds., *Handbook of Aging*, 255–56; Streib, "Social Stratification and Aging."
30. Tamir, *Communication and the Aging Process*, 126.
31. Irving Rosow, "Housing and Local Ties of the Aged," in *Middle Age and Aging*, ed. Bernice L. Neugarten (Chicago: University of Chicago Press, 1968), 382–89.

32. Tamir, *Communication and the Aging Process*, 130.
33. See Marjorie F. Lowenthal and Clayton Haven, "Interaction and Adaptation: Intimacy as a Critical Variable," *American Sociological Review* 33 (February 1968): 20–30.
34. Tamir, *Communication and the Aging Process*, 132, citing Irving Rosow, *Social Integration of the Aged* (New York: Free Press, 1967) and "Housing and Local Ties of the Aged," in Neugarten, ed., *Middle Age and Aging*.
35. Gerard Egan, *The Skilled Helper: A Systematic Approach to Effective Helping* (Pacific Grove, Calif.: Brooks/Cole, 1986), 59–66.
36. Ibid., 60.
37. Ibid., 64, citing Jack R. Gibb, *Trust: A New View of Personal and Organizational Development* (Los Angeles: The Guild of Tutors Press, 1978).

CHAPTER

# 8

# Institutional Response to Informational Need

We will analyze the impact of institutions on informational transfer by studying four principal types of institutions in our society: the church, educational institutions, libraries, and the government. Each analysis will seek to make the point that information is a prime mover regardless of the type of program/service with which the institution is primarily concerned.

## Getting Information from the Church/Synagogue

Let us categorize the information that the church and synagogue can provide into two distinct types: (1) personal information, or the emphasis upon the questions that any individual elder is likely to have and to seek religious understanding about; and (2) "group" information, or the emphasis upon spiritual understanding that can be provided by the church. This section will discuss each in turn.

### *Personal Information*

No institution in society is more suited or has a longer history in answering the "big" questions in life than the church or synagogue. Why am I here? What is life all about? Is this all there is? Does life go on beyond the grave? No less a psychological giant than Carl Jung himself indicated that most psychological questioning beyond age thirty-five is essentially religious in nature.[1] By going on to point out that no lasting psychological improvement occurred *except when* an individual regained a religious attitude toward life, we see the tremendous value of religion in the later years highlighted. What is true, in Jung's view, for anyone past age thirty-five, seems at least doubly true for individuals age sixty-five and older. We turn to the church often when we are in need of support and understanding; the information (guidance) that the church/synagogue can offer is well-nigh impossible to find outside its walls. What secular institution would seek to provide solace as one's spouse was dying? Or to provide answers when one's own death seems ever-nearing and can no longer be seen as a mere abstraction, to be thrust into the distant future?

Many elders do look to the church/synagogue for just such information in their declining years. There is a greater tie to the church than to any other institution, and although there is no perceived link between mere church attendance and well-being in the final years, a link has been demonstrated between spiritual understanding—"faith," if you will—and personal well-being in the latter years. An early comprehensive study found that "believers" had an average personal adjustment score of 27.2, and "nonbelievers," 19.9—a statistically significant difference.[2] Why this is so really takes little analysis. For those who can accept the church/synagogue's answers, there is great value in finding surety about life's ultimate questions when facing the final riddle of death. This is the information about which the individual is most likely to need help, including, and perhaps especially significantly, when these questions have not been addressed satisfactorily in earlier years. One can postpone uncertainties only so long, and the aging person has come up against postponement for the last time. It behooves the church/synagogue to offer intellectually and emotionally satisfying answers to these mystical questions, because if it fails to deliver where it is most suited—the question of God—then group programs will not suffice. The church/synagogue will have failed at what it alone can do best.

### *Group Activities*

This category is the church/synagogue's so-called "social gospel"—doing unto others through service. In this area, the church can best be an adjunct to official social programs carried out by others, because personnel are generally limited and administrative experience short, among the volunteers to whom the church must turn for such programs. The church/synagogue simply does not have the financial resources to be the network for real social and economic need among elders. Historically, the church has served as a support in times of crisis, and can continue to do so with success. But when long-term need takes over, the task is best left to other institutions. We have become such a secular society that any attempt by churches to provide for nonmembers as well as members would raise the charge that they are not taking care of their own. And any attempt to solely "take care of their own" would mean that many non–church related individuals would be left alone in time of need. The all-pervasive nature of the church in medieval times simply has no parallel in present-day society. The church can serve informally as an informational transfer agency, though, in that it is highly decentralized, and clergy are likely to know of needs within their congregations. Because numerically, membership in the church is greater than membership in any other institution, then the church faithful have yet another avenue for satisfying their information-gathering needs. One does not ever "retire" from church, of course; even the shut-in can keep some contact, as visitation from the clergy is a staple of the ongoing ministry of the church to its members.

A 1982 study indicated that those who serve the informational needs of the aging in various capacities (librarians, gerontologists in provider network, etc.) believed that the church was about midway (nineteenth) in importance among some forty items listed as prospective informational transfer agents.[3] A follow-up study found that the elderly themselves believed that the church's importance in informational transfer was even greater; they ranked it third in importance among these same forty ways of receiving information.[4] This spotlights the importance of the church in informational transfer, as perceived by the aging themselves. There are some indications, such as a much-touted National Symposium on the Church and Aging in 1984, which suggest that religious institutions are beginning to respond to the challenge.

## Getting Information from the School

Education for older adults has had something of an identity crisis for as long as this issue has been around, but thankfully the question appears to be emerging well and strong. It represents the systematic gathering of information in an institutional context. At the crux of the matter is the usually unspoken issue of "Why educate at all?" As a society that determines worth on the basis of goods and services rendered, we have silently questioned the value of providing educational opportunities for that segment of our population who will die sooner than the rest of us. What good would it do to educate elders and have them take their newfound knowledge to the grave? Because this opinion is so crass, it has remained largely a quiet issue but has nevertheless created ambivalence at the center of education for the aging. Only recently has a philosophy of educational gerontology emerged that offers a reason to educate the aging on the basis of both individual need as well as desire, and on the basis of the value-added contribution of elders that will accrue to society at large. As Lowy and O'Connor indicate, the well-being of both individuals and society will be enhanced.[5] This new view is a result, in part, of the relatively new belief that the best life for elders is an active and involved one; the old "disengagement" theories are seen negatively. Moreover, education in general is being seen as a lifelong enterprise, rather than one limited to the early years. The 1971 White House Conference on Aging passed a resolution declaring that education is a basic right for all groups, and the delegates followed up with a comprehensive list of recommendations that, if implemented, would ensure this right. The United Nations-sponsored World Assembly on Aging (1982) recommended that "education must be made available without discrimination against the elderly." With statements such as those announcing direction, and with older adults developing greater clout as their numbers increase, there can now be less concern that any elder's right to education will be silenced.

This is not to say, though, that barriers do not exist. Patricia Cross (1979) has identified three types of barriers: situational, dispositional, and institutional.[6] Let us examine each in turn.

Situational barriers exist because of the particular life situation of the elder; as identified by Cross, these include cost, transportation, and restrictions because of physical handicaps or poor health. Cross also cites lack of time, energy, and financial resources. She recommends such changes as making transportation available and reducing expense for those who enroll. (The latter, in practice, is more common than the former.)

Dispositional barriers are attitudinal restrictions placed on activity, particularly lack of interest or feeling too old to learn. Johnstone and Rivera believe that these attitudes may be more common than we know.[7] The aging probably feel that being "uninterested" in education is a socially unacceptable attitude, and as a result may give other reasons (notably situational) to explain why they do not partake of educational opportunities. This attitudinal factor is more difficult to combat than the others. If elders do not view educational opportunities as a strong plus for them, they will never take advantage in any great numbers. Some of the old stereotypes may come into play here: being "too old to learn" is one of the most common. While an elder may not actually *believe* this myth, he or she may feel inferior because of limited opportunity in education at an earlier date, and may feel that it is "too late" to remedy that now. Also, many much younger people who have been out of school for fifteen years or more are extremely reluctant to put their "rusty" skills to the test, and express disinterest because of fear; the aging are prone to this same negative view. Insofar as possible, any education that seeks to become attractive to the aging person must be as nonthreatening as possible. In planning for such experiences, it is good to include older adults, who will be cognizant of the barriers. As elders actually enroll and experience the positive benefits, others will be encouraged as well. Acceptance is one of the qualities that appears most important.[8]

Finally, institutional barriers are very real barriers and usually result in elders' reticence. Although this is changing, the rules for getting an education are geared to the younger generation, and often do not "fit" the elder's more relaxed life-style. There are matters of inconvenient scheduling and registration procedures, inaccessible buildings, and the lack of counseling and financial aid. More emphasis must also be placed upon outreach; the aging do usually sign up as readily as younger people do. With the emphasis now on lifelong learning, however, many changes are occurring that will prove beneficial to the older learner. Sometimes the site should be one with which the elder is more comfortable, such as a senior center or library. One program that has proved to be a major success, because it takes the elder where he or she is, and builds upon it, is Elderhostel. Because this program has, from the outset, been geared to aging interests and aging needs, it has not suffered from the influence of the younger generation on its design.

McClusky grouped the educational needs of the aging into five categories: coping needs, expressive needs, contributive needs, influence needs, and transcendental needs.[9] While McClusky indicated that this order is from most important to least, Lowy and O'Connor disagree, saying that individual order of importance is likely to differ. This is probably because the aging, perhaps even more so than other groups, are quite diverse in outlook and experience. Let us take a look at each category in turn.

### *Coping Needs*

Most older adults have already demonstrated their ability to cope; simply growing older does not limit this life skill, although one may be required to draw upon coping reserves more so than before, as age and illness take their toll. There are a couple of factors that impinge upon this ability: the lower educational attainment and basic literacy of elders vis-à-vis groups of younger people; and the fast pace of society today, which by constantly changing is apt to challenge even the hardiest younger person. The literate elder is likely to be substantially more autonomous than the illiterate, in part because in today's society the regulations of the government influence the day-to-day lives of the aging. (Social Security and Medicare are the most readily apparent examples of this influence.) Someone must interpret the rules that determine financial considerations for the elderly, and if the elder does not read well or is illiterate, he or she is dependent upon others for this difficult task. Closely related are the many other facts of daily living that are in flux. Because the retired elder is apt to be more disengaged from the mainstream than when working, he or she must take special steps to keep up. Younger family members and friends can be particularly helpful. Both of these points suggest the need for practical life skills on the part of the aging, and education can fulfill this need.

### *Contributory Needs*

An older adult needs and wants to be needed and generally still has the potential to contribute. Meaningful contributions will go a long way toward diminishing any sense of being superfluous in society. Frequently, but not always, the service will be voluntary. These activities emphasize the service potential of the elderly. As time goes by, more and more programs of this type are established, a phenomenon attributable to the success of current programs. What are some of the more successful? Lowy and O'Connor cite the National Retired Teachers Association/American Association of Retired Persons' program of peer counselors to help other recently widowed persons cope with grief and attendant experiences. ACTION, a federal governmental agency, sponsors the "Foster Grandparents Program." Several programs not generally thought of as aging involvements, but which employ substantial numbers of the elder population, are the Peace Corps and VISTA (Volunteers in Service to America). And intergenerational programs are also coming into their own as aging becomes recognized as a phenomenon that affects all of society. Libraries are frequently the site of such programs. A successful program does not have to be national in scope to attract a loyal following. Community-based programs are equally needed, and in some cases may be more successful because of their intimate knowledge of the aging population in a given area.

### *Influencing Needs*

This is one of the areas that has the most potential, a fact that has been alluded to earlier. The number of older adults is growing rapidly, and efforts to organize for influence and advocacy of older adults' concerns have become more widespread. The most successful lobbying effort for the aging portion of society is arguably the American Association for Retired Persons (AARP). Another highly successful group that made the news more frequently a few years ago is the Gray Panthers. These groups are professional in outlook and have developed clout as spokespersons for the aging. The AARP, in particular, would like to be recognized as representing all older persons. With groups such as these becoming more and more active, there is less need to be concerned that the aging will be unfairly treated in the future, a charge that is frequently made and certainly cannot be disputed as having some basis in fact. As elders have become savvy about politicking for themselves, there may be some backlash from younger voters, but none of us would go back to the days of a weaker, often voiceless, older generation.

### *Transcendental Needs*

As in Maslow's hierarchy, it is unlikely that these needs will be met until more fundamental coping needs have been met; but once the lower-order needs are satisfied, the elder, like all others who are younger, will seek to satisfy the longings of the soul. Aesthetic needs may be expressed in painting or sculpture—activities for which some education may be in order; frequently, the elder may engage in these activities for the first time at an advanced age. Sometimes elders review their lives, quietly or in group discussion. Library programs often encourage this, as the highly acclaimed and popular "Bi-Folkal" kits make possible. Aging individuals are encouraged to relive their past as a means to integrate their experiences into their present lives. Some of these transcendental needs relate to an aging person's realization that time is fleeting and that death will come. Various educational programs can be designed to assist older individuals to deal concretely with this concept and to face it without pain.

Consequently, we can see that there are a variety of barriers to educational opportunities for the typical elderly person. One must be somewhat proactive to actually take advantage of the programs that are available. It is hoped that this situation will improve in future years, when elders will come to their advanced age from a better-educated past, making them more likely to continue to advance intellectually. Once the decision is made to seek education, in whatever form, one will note that the types of needs to be satisfied are as diverse as for any other age group, and possibly more so. They range from the most mundane coping skills to the most sublime questions of life and death. Given this diversity, it is no surprise that the educational programs themselves need to exist in a variety of settings and need to be sponsored by a variety of groups. Once an elder has had a successful educational experience, he or she is far more likely to seek out such experience later on. Success builds, and an educated citizenry is the result. Certainly all of us must do what we can to ensure that all segments of our population benefit from as much education as they are willing and able to receive.

## Getting Information from the Library

For several years culminating in 1987, a committee of the American Library Association charged with services to the aging worked diligently to compile a set of guidelines on library service to older adults. The new document superceded guidelines that had been adopted in 1975. When completed by the Reference and Adult Services (RASD) Library Service to an Aging Population Committee, the set of twelve recommendations (each having several sub-recommendations) was distributed widely and received much press in library publications.[10] These guidelines, like virtually all guidelines adopted by ALA, are meant to serve as targets for service, not minimum standards for service. The "Guidelines for Library Service to Older Adults" are what libraries would seek to do under the best of conditions (optimal funding, sufficient staffing, etc.). No library could boast of successfully fulfilling all recommendations, but many librarians interested in providing the best service to the aging do read the guidelines with a view to upgrading their service to this constituency. Let us take a look at what library service for the aging should look like by using these guidelines as the basis for discussion.

The first recommendation is for a positive attitude toward the elderly and the aging process itself; i.e., "*Exhibit and promote a positive attitude toward the aging process and older adults*." The guidelines begin with this imperative in part because librarians are, unfortunately, often just as likely as any other group to fail to view aging in positive terms. Kenneth Ferstl determined in doctoral research published in 1977 that individual librarians sometimes did subscribe to popular stereotypes and misconceptions, although as a group they strongly subscribed to library documents (then in effect) that gave solid support to serving the elderly in meaningful ways.[11] Gerontologists and others interested in serving the aging have also noted that some individuals hesitate to study aging formally and to devote their professional lives to the aging because they feel threatened by the aging process; it reminds them of their own mortality. Consequently, sub-recommendations that elucidate this first item include a call for improved communication and for more education (including continuing education) about aging as a process throughout the lifespan, a denunciation of stereotypical thinking and labeling, and an imperative to exhibit the same degree of interest and respect for older adults as for any other patrons.

A second component of this first recommendation was a tacit acknowledgment that many of the services to the aging provided by libraries have historically been for the homebound, who frequently are impaired elderly rather than individuals still able to pursue an active life. This linkage between aging and illness is unfortunate, and while the programs that have historically served the aging are laudatory, many more elders would be potential patrons of library programs that undergird an active life-style.

The second recommendation is a broad statement of intent to provide information and resources about aging to any potential library clientele who may be interested in older adults: "*Promote information and resources on aging and its implications not only to older adults themselves but also to family members, professionals in the field of aging, and other persons interested in the aging process*." Much information relevant to the mission of the library in regard to elders is embodied in this recommendation. The library collection on the aging should be designed to meet the needs of clientele who will be doing diverse things—study/education to understand the aging process, planning for a change in life-style (frequently because of retirement), advocacy, offering service directly to the aging (by "service providers"), the provision of information on disabilities that would answer many current concerns, and learning about the "potential for growth over the lifespan." Specifically, selection and weeding of the book collection will ensure that the books and other materials are up-to-date on such issues as lifelong learning; older adults as consumers of aging services; behavioral implications of being older; cultural, ethnic, etc., differences among the aging; leisure-time activities; and what has become known as the issue of the "graying of America," i.e., the aging of our population. Library collections should be well selected to include large-print books, audiovisuals, etc.—formats that will enhance access for the minority of elderly who have impairments. The library should not, however, just stay within its four walls. Information should be available about gerontological resources in the community, community agencies that serve the aging, and activities for the aging within the community. An information-and-referral service to address aging concerns is recommended. And, finally, all of these resources provided by the library should be adequately publicized to ensure their appropriate utilization.

The third recommendation is a call for diversity, but before this term had been generally accepted to reflect an appreciation for ethnic, cultural, and economic differences. The guideline reads: "*Assure services for older adults which reflect cultural, ethnic and economic differences.*" The library service provided to older adults should be cognizant of such differences and reflect a positive regard for them. Not only should the service be sensitive to diversity, but the collections should also reflect the varying backgrounds that readers bring to the library. The lower literacy rate of elders who are minorities is also a concern. Librarians are exhorted to become knowledgeable about these differences, and to use this information to add to the collection appropriately, to train staff, to offer suitable programming that will attract diverse clientele, and to cooperate with other agencies in so doing. Literacy was highlighted finally as a concern, probably because some minorities have had less opportunity to learn in an optimal environment than other Americans have.

Fourth is a recommendation to be sensitive to the minority of older adults who are isolated, homebound, institutionalized, or disabled: "*Provide library service appropriate to the special needs of all older adults, including the minority who are geographically isolated, homebound, institutionalized, or disabled.*" This guideline is phrased very carefully (note the word "minority"), because these attributes are all too often stereotypes of *all* aging people. Identified as responding to "special needs," this guideline calls for trained staff to work with individuals having these needs, special materials (large-print books, talking books, magnifying devices, page turners, etc.) to assist elders who have disabilities, personalized library service (sometimes on-site to the homebound or institutionalized), and cooperation with the staff of institutions to plan appropriate library service. Individuals with these special needs should be first identified, and then service specific to the given disability must be devised. This guideline recognizes that disabilities are extremely diverse, sometimes coming more than one at a time, and as a result, the type of service to be offered must, in some cases, be unique to the individual. This guideline was edited carefully by librarians who were members of the division of the American Library Association that serves these special needs: the Association of Specialized and Cooperative Library Agencies (ASCLA), specifically the Library Service to the Impaired Elderly Forum (LSIEF) within that division.

The fifth recommendation would utilize the service of elders to be liaisons to their peers and to serve as resources in intergenerational programming. It reads, "*Utilize the potential of older adults (paid or volunteer) as liaisons to reach their peers and as a resource in intergenerational programming.*" This guideline asserts that the library has an obligation to enlist the cooperation of the aging themselves in planning programs and developing resources for their age group. When this is not done (e.g., elders are not consulted), and a program fails to ignite interest, librarians are then set up to wonder, in the dark, just why. Elders assisting in this way should be both volunteer and paid; the guideline was worded in this way out of awareness that funds will not always be available for paid work, but that paying for their work is optimal. We should not take advantage of the elderly by using their expertise only when it is offered free of charge. Specific components of their assistance would include training regular library staff to work with the aging and keeping staff informed of aging concerns.

The sixth guideline continues the emphasis upon paid work for the aging by stating directly, "*Employ older adults at both professional and support levels for either general library work or for programs specifically targeted to older adults.*" One of the sub-recommendations makes clear the intent by stating explicitly, "Request volunteer help only when funding is not available for paid positions." The only other sub-recommendation to this guideline is a call for nondiscrimination in hiring the elderly. Since this guideline went into effect, society as a whole has become much more cognizant of age discrimination, and has taken legal steps to curtail it. By denouncing age discrimination, this guideline anticipated the rest of society, legally, and was pro-active morally for a more open society for elders. The fact that this guideline recognizes the contributions of elders to general library work, rather than just in services to the elderly, is a positive aspect worth noting.

The need for community programming is highlighted in the seventh guideline: "*Involve older adults in the planning and design of library services and programs for the entire community and for older adults in particular.*" This guideline spotlights a need, long recognized by librarians, for social responsibility in reaching out to those who do not, of their own volition, find their way into the library. A sub-recommendation asks for a needs assessment among older adults in the community; this underscores the necessity to make programs and other services responsive to real problems and interests. After identifying older adults who will participate in such planning, librarians are actually to put the plan into action. Like any other group, librarians may develop grandiose plans, only to see few of them actually become reality, and the wording of this guideline is developed in such a way as to negate this tendency. Successful library programs have borne out the truth that involvement of the aging is necessary to successful planning; otherwise, the planning takes place in a vacuum, and the programs are likely to be poorly received by elders.

The library's need for greater cooperation with other agencies that serve the aging is emphasized in the eighth guideline: "*Promote and develop working relationships with other agencies and groups connected with the needs of older adults.*" This need was recognized in a Delphi study carried out a decade ago as one of the principal ways to enhance informational dispersal among the aging.[12] Since any given agency cannot be all things to all people, the best means of meeting informational (as well as other) needs is through greater cooperation among agencies who have an interest as well as a responsibility to the aging. We must first identify those agencies, and then sit down with their personnel to plan ways in which libraries can contribute to the overall satisfaction of elders' needs. In addition to agencies employed to assist the elders, this planning should expand to include cooperation with organizations whose membership *is* the elderly. Finally, this cooperation should include networking among librarians "belonging" to different libraries. Cooperative collection development (the purchasing of books and other materials), and services and programming that complement (rather than compete with) each other are recommended. The final sub-recommendation in this area is a call for comprehensive cooperative planning: lifelong learning opportunities, pre-retirement groups, minimized duplication of services, greater information-and-referral services to elders, and greater awareness on the part of professionals who deal with the aging by keeping abreast of current developments in aging.

Pre-retirement planning, first mentioned above, is given its own guideline: "*Provide programs, services, and information for those preparing for retirement or later-life career alternatives.*" It is made clear that this period of life may be a contrast to what has gone before, but it may only be a shift in emphasis, not a true "retirement." This ninth guideline's sub-recommendations focus on collections, bibliographies, seminars (or other programming), etc. The possibility is also raised that the library can serve as a clearinghouse for information on retirement and alternative career choices for the elderly.

The next guideline implicitly and explicitly focuses on the special needs that some older adults have: Disabilities may hinder access to the library. The tenth guideline reads, "*Facilitate library use by older persons through improved library design and access to transportation.*" The same Delphi study mentioned above saw transportation as the number one barrier to access to information needed by elders to function successfully in society.[13] (Other studies have consistently found this to be true.) As mentioned earlier, the ALA Library Services to the Impaired Elderly Forum edited these guidelines for maximum impact toward meeting these special needs. The collections and meeting rooms must be physically accessible, various "assistive" devices should be provided to the handicapped, signage should be large-print, etc. Of course, funding for this must be forthcoming if the library is to adapt, and federal funding is now mandated by law for adjustments in the physical environment of institutions such as the library for elders who have special needs.

We have earlier mentioned a needs assessment as a viable way to determine what types of services should be offered to elders. This method is given its own guideline, number eleven, which reads as follows: "*Incorporate as part of the library's planning and evaluation process the changing needs of an aging population.*" The sub-recommendations make clear that a formal needs assessment is what the writers of this document had in mind. The changing needs of elders are highlighted, and librarians must regularly test the waters to be sure that we are providing what is needed. This guideline emphasizes with the term, "changing needs," the "graying" of the population. It is virtually impossible to read any article discussing the needs of older people without encountering a statistical profile emphasizing that their numbers are larger, both as a percentage of the total population and in the aggregate, and these figures are expected to climb into the next century rapidly. The "graying" should be a call for action on our part.

Finally, the all-important fact of funding is directly addressed in the twelfth guideline: "*Aggressively seek sources of funding and commit a portion of the library budget to programs and services for older adults.*" The writers meant the guideline to read as assertively as possible and chose the word, "aggressively," deliberately. All too often librarians, as befitting their stereotype, have stepped back timidly when requests were denied; this guideline asserts the necessity never to take "no" for an answer if that answer can be turned into a "maybe" or a "yes." This is especially true if funds are available, but a louder voice places them in another program, serving different clientele. It is implicitly recognized in the wording of this guideline that things will remain the same unless librarians are willing to fight for what they believe in; if greater services for the aging are as needed as these committed librarians believe, then we must truly do all that we can to ensure that funding will increase to supply the needs that elders have in regard to library services and collections. The library can serve optimally as a nonthreatening place for gathering information; many will, for example, learn to read in a library, whereas they would be more hesitant to go to a school. This idea serves for many other services that can legitimately be provided as well.

### *Summary*

Librarians have, through the years, not done enough for elders within the walls of libraries. But such staff cannot allow this to continue if their job is to be done right. Library services and programs to elders will become more and more important as the years go by. As elders increase in numbers, their advocacy will increase, and other agencies will step in to provide the services, probably for a fee. The library is uniquely suited for providing the informational undergirding of our society—a role that sometimes only librarians take seriously. Librarians and library staff need to move with the times, energetically embracing the information age that so many are talking about. This speaks to elders as well, even if they have not been lifelong users of the library. Let those in charge of libraries reach for the funding, and carefully budget what is available now, to provide for the informational needs of this increasingly able and active generation of older adults.

Acting upon these guidelines will not help every elderly person who has the need for greater access to information, because there are constraints in funding and personnel that make the issues bigger than can be addressed conclusively. But the library can make a new beginning, and that effort might turn out to be far better than we might hope now.

## Getting Information about Governmental Programs and Services

The federal government's Administration on Aging (AOA), created by the Older Americans Act (OAA) of 1965 (and amended many times since), is the focal point for coordination and implementation of the nation's many governmental programs and services for the aging. Many of these programs are housed in other agencies, and some, such as the Social Security Administration, far predate the OAA. Moreover, to a large extent, because of the characteristics of the network that have been set up, this federal office affects greatly the programs and services for the aging as carried out by state and local governments as well.

The fact that there are so many programs and that their administration, although coordinated to an extent by the AOA, is in actuality dispersed among numerous agencies, is a major reason that informational needs of older adults can be so great. As people age, they may have greater need for social services, even though they may *not* be living in poverty. (For individuals who live in poverty, the needs are frequently greater.) And older adults may be at a disadvantage in finding out what programs and services are available. Complexity is also simply greater in our 1990s world, and the world of governmental programs and services may appear to be a maze that is well-nigh impossible to navigate. What has been done about this problem?

In 1973, almost a decade after the Older Americans Act was enacted, Congress passed legislation (as amendments to this act) that mandated the development of information and referral programs for the elderly. This was, in fact, to be given priority by the network on aging emanating from the Administration on Aging. The reason? Surveys had revealed that only a small percentage of elderly people were taking advantage of services for which they were legitimately eligible. Why? Not because of reticence in being involved with social programs (although this has undoubtedly been a factor for some elderly), but because they did not know that the service existed! Primary to the mission of the network on aging, therefore, was the Administration on Aging's coordinating responsibility within the federal government, coupled with the influence that the federal involvements would have on state and local policies.

To address this now-recognized need, information-and-referral services, dubbed "I&R," were set up in various settings and under various jurisdictions. Frequently, though, this service is one of the few that is administered directly either by a state unit on aging (SUA), or one of the 650-plus local Area Agencies on Aging (AAAs) that are part of the network. (Most of the other programs and services in the network are on a contract basis.)[14]

### *Information and Referral Services*

What exactly does I&R do for the aging individual? The answers vary almost as much as the services themselves, which can be noted for their diversity.[15] The primary purpose is to link the older adult to the service that he or she needs because of an expressed problem. If a caller just asks a question, and receives information, but contact is *never* made with the service point, the case can be made that I&R truly failed. The informational need must connect with the service designed to provide a benefit. Only then can success be measured.

At the federal level, I&R services are shared among the Administration on Aging, the Social Security Administration, and the Community Services Administration. State and county social service organizations also do their part. Finally, at the community level, a wide variety of public and private organizations serve an informational function relative to the aging. The staff serving at this reference point are supposed to be skilled enough in social service work to ask the right questions—first. Does the individual, for example, have anyone to whom he or she can turn for rudimentary assistance in answering the need? (Presumably the whole problem cannot be solved by this individual, or it might have already been solved without the phone call.) It is generally recognized that learning the context of the problem is necessary before rushing in with aid that may hurt or hinder rather than help. Then the staff of the I&R must have up-to-date files and knowledge of those files that will enable them to make the appropriate linkage. (Computerization has not yet been utilized to the extent it should be, because of low funding; but the potential for highly sophisticated systems is present.) The staff should know the great variety of services available, and skillfully negotiate the delivery of those services to the people who need them. For this, a resources file must be compiled that includes the following, as outlined by Harbert and Ginsberg: (1) name, address, phone number of agency or organization providing the given service; (2) the nature, amount, and duration of the service being provided; (3) the criteria that must be met by the individual seeking to make use of this aid; (4) the name of a current contact person within the agency. In the course of studying this detailed data (which must be kept *current*—a task in and of itself), the staff of the I&R must make crucial decisions about what service is appropriate in light of the given need. They may call on virtually anybody anywhere. Such service, as we have perhaps implied, is by no means limited to governmental help via social service agencies that serve the aging; private agencies, businesses, and community organizations are also to be called upon.[16]

Ultimately, as we have noted, the task of the I&R is not complete until the individual who has sought information from the I&R actually makes the connection with the agency recommended as having a solution to the problem. As Huttman states, a good information and referral service "does more: it negotiates the client's use of the program and assures his accessibility to it."[17] If a client, for example, uses *only* I&R, the "end is not achieved, for the needed service is not used."[18] Consequently, follow-up to such calls should be a necessary part of the evaluative process of the I&R function. Unfortunately, in the rush of trying to provide much service with limited staffing, this need frequently goes unmet.

An I&R service can be the "first stop" for individuals in need. This fact makes the service of crucial importance. If the staff is inadequately trained, more harm than good can result. This fact is one of the greatest problems for I&R services; the skills demanded are so great, and the pay is frequently inadequate. Skills in counseling are heavily needed, and the agency may not be able to attract staff who have this very important background.

In order for the I&R service to *be* the "first step," though, individuals must first know about it. In a survey compiled in 1980–81, this author found that public relations was one of the services most necessary for agencies on aging, but also one of the most difficult to implement.[19] There is evidence that those most in need of an I&R service are the *least* likely to call, largely because they are not aware of the I&R's existence. A few years ago, Battle & Associates found that isolated and unattached elders remained unattached to this service, as they did to most other services that are potentially available.[20] At that time, only 66 percent of I&Rs tried to solve this problem by providing outreach and case-finding services. The main problem was lack of funding.

How, in fact, *do* agencies such as I&R "get the word out" about what they do? By a wide variety of information-dispersal techniques, with the mass media being the first choice (although frequently one of the most expensive). Spots on radio or television would be optimal, but all too often the agency has to settle for less-visible means—newspaper features from time to time and announcements in periodicals and other publications read by the aging. The governmental pages of the phone books are an obvious necessity, and an avenue that is routinely used. Unfortunately, there is great evidence that the "unconnected" elderly, who may be in greatest need, are the least likely to know about I&R.

Coordination between information-and-referral offices and various other service agencies often falls short of the optimum. Centralization of services may lose some of the grass-roots dimension of good I&R, but if there is little or no centralization, the service itself may be poor. There are no easy answers. In many respects, the difficulties that I&R services for the aging have encountered are emblematic of the great difficulties in informational transfer among people in general, and especially the aging. These agencies have been addressing the problem since 1973 in some fashion (and before that in various, less-formal ways), and the problem of informational receipt by clients in need is still very much apparent.

## *Types of Governmental Programs/Services*

We have frequently made the point that any problem is at base an informational need: to solve the problem, we must first get information on *how* to solve it. What types of governmental programs and services do the elderly need to know about? What exists for their benefit? We will take a quick overview of programs and services, by categories, about which more information is usually needed. These programs and services are government's answers to solving problems—the means by which we as a people, through our government, have found to address need among the elderly. We will use the outline of Gelfand as a point of departure.[21] We have already discussed his first category of programs for the aging—information and referral, or I&R.

### Health and Mental Health

The system of governmental support for ill health is highly visible through Medicare and Medicaid programs, both of which support the elderly, depending upon degree of need. Medicare, originating in 1965, has taken away some of the worry of growing ill in the later years; but when this care, to which all older citizens are entitled, proves not to be enough and personal resources have been depleted, Medicaid—health services for the financially needy—takes over. The vast cost of health care in this country and the fact that the elderly are more prone to health problems than any other age group have combined to create a specter of fear for an entire population of people. This has led to the movement to expand Medicare benefits to cover some catastrophic health costs, which were passed by Congress and signed by President Reagan in 1988; this was the first major enhancement of Medicare benefits since their inception. Despite much criticism that the bill did not go far enough, it attempted through compromise between the legislative and executive branches to find some solution to the questions asked by most elderly in regard to long-term disability: What will I do if I become ill and must use all my savings? How will my family and I be cared for in that situation? Because Medicare's current solution to this problem is only partial (by any account), the fear of growing old and perhaps sustaining poor health has not abated, with good reason, among most seniors. And so the debate about catastrophic health insurance continues. At this writing, the Clinton administration is studying the issue for our society as a whole.

Certainly the fact that these governmental programs exist in all of their complexity creates an informational need that is not easily addressed. The rules change, the forms are hard to fill out (and may be in small print as well, compounding sight problems among some elderly), and a minimal level of education is almost mandatory to understanding one's entitlements. In such a situation, the person is also suffering from a health problem, and the last thing he or she needs is more hassle to add to an already burdensome and probably fearful health condition. Most individuals prefer to remain autonomous, but this is one area in which one may be forced to depend upon others to provide answers to what is fundamentally an informational need.

Because the rules are so complex and change so frequently, the people to whom one turns may not be knowledgeable as well. And so the older person may be trapped. Mistakes may be made in understanding one's entitlements to which redress is often difficult or impossible; the elder may not even realize that the mistake has been made, given the fact that he or she has had to depend upon others to give the proper information. This scenario certainly paints old age at one of its most vulnerable points, and there is no way to solve the problem—yet. Society *must* be made cognizant of the very real problems inherent in poor health among the aging, and must seek solutions to address informational, as well as other, problems inherent in these dilemmas.

How might this problem be addressed? It is probably a dead end to suggest that the laws be made less complicated. Certainly the *explanations* can be improved, and should be, but there are good reasons for the complexities in a complex situation, and a minimal level of education is almost mandatory to understanding the regulations. Compromise in the process of passing the laws makes the complexity greater—a necessary evil to the greater good of passing any helpful laws at all. The best solution is more and better trained informational consultants, possibly governmental but certainly better compensated. As we noted in discussing I&R, positions such as these are notorious in their low status and low pay, and, as a result, individuals are hired who will stay on the job only a short time, virtually ensuring that they are likely to leave just as adequate competence is gained. As anyone in the information business would readily recognize, having good sources of information (in this case a knowledgeable, well-compensated, long-term employee) is essential to the dispensation of such information.

### Transportation

In virtually any survey of the needs of elders, adequate transportation ranks at or near the top of the list. Visual problems preclude many elders from driving, especially at night, and even the best-designed mass transit system may not meet the real need of elders for maintaining relationships with family and friends. In a city, the chances of a good transportation system are, of course, tremendously enhanced, but suburban or rural living usually precludes any independence in regard to transportation for the elderly who no longer drive. The wave of the future is minibus and van systems, many equipped for wheelchairs. A major question, as yet unresolved, is whether or not such transit will be age-segregated; this is a legal question that has no easy answer, given complicated contractual agreements between private bus lines and governmental agencies. For the future, we need to ensure that medical needs and shopping needs are answered via appropriate transportation, at least in urban areas. Realistically, the more isolated elderly will continue to depend upon significant others to supply much in the way of transportation needs.

Transportation does not, in and of itself, appear to be very information-bound. But a panel of Delphi experts listed the availability of transportation as number one in a list of informational-gathering techniques.[22] The question was worded in such a way as to recognize a way for elders to reach information-gathering programs and services. Elders agreed with this assessment.[23]

### Crime and Legal Assistance Programs

We have earlier made the point that the elderly feel especially vulnerable to crime, and as a result may not go outside in the evening or venture too far from home. Actual statistics do not show that the elderly are more prone to victimization than any other age group; in fact, the statistics are disproportionately low. This may be misleading, however, in that the habits of the elderly, chosen out of fear, may serve as protection. If one is not out on the streets at night, obviously the crime statistics will not list elders as victims during that highly vulnerable time of the day. Because the elder's fear is generally great, in part because of physical incapacity or slowness to react and get out of the way, educational programs need to be carried out that target the elderly in regard to ways that they can protect themselves. Some are in place, including especially efforts by the AARP. These educational programs focus on how to avoid street crimes (theft is predominantly the crime of choice against the elderly) and how to recognize confidence games. Other educational programs focus on crime prevention by encouraging greater cohesiveness in the community. Finally, there may be special "victim assistance" programs that aid the elderly once a crime has been committed.[24] Here we see that greater information offered via educational endeavors serves to meet the elderly's need, even though the problem cannot be eliminated. It can be reduced.

### Employment and Volunteer Work

Not every elder looks forward to retirement, a truism that society has, belatedly, moved to remedy. If the elder is willing and able to work, both paid and volunteer employment are options. In some cases, appraisal must be done to determine feasibility of particular kinds of employment, and this can include counseling and testing. As the laws on making money have eased, elders are able to continue to receive their full entitlement under Social Security, regardless of employment status. If a "regular" job is not appropriate (for whatever reason), volunteer work is an option that society has been trying to encourage. We must be sure never to take advantage of the skills of elders by refusing to pay when remuneration is possible, a fact that libraries have become particularly sensitive to (as seen above in the *Guidelines*). But the fact remains that the needs of our society are so great, particularly in one-to-one settings, that the extra hands and minds of elderly people can make a substantial difference in serving people's needs—including informational needs that would otherwise go unmet. In our society today, many people feel that we simply cannot afford to meet many needs—particularly social service needs—totally with paid employees. Greater assistance in these areas by motivated volunteers would be a very real contribution on the part of the aging, and this fact should be recognized and addressed. Much of such social services assistance that is needed is of a quasi-educational, or informational, nature. One direct example is serving literacy needs, a task that calls for one-on-one assistance. In looking at the total picture, though, the elderly could provide the personal element in our social programs, whether governmentally based or private. "Being there" to provide support, the elder would frequently respond by providing additional information about the situation that the individual in need is facing. Because elders have the advantage of experience, their contributions can be in areas that they have already lived through themselves. Hospital volunteers are an obvious example of the type of support that this line of reasoning suggests. In this example, rather than being on the receiving end of information (which has been our focus), the elder is actually providing it; but the benefits of the exchange would surely accrue to him or her as well.

### Nutrition Programs

These programs were mandated at the federal level, and as a result the guidelines have been clearer here than for certain other programs.[25] An important component of the program has been the fact that all elders are welcomed, and an effort is made to avoid the appearance of "charity," which is rejected by many elders. (Program centers are, however, more often placed in low-income areas, where the need is presumed to be greater.) Two general types of programs are available: a nutrition site to which elders congregate for the noon meal; or "Meals-on-Wheels," the prepared meal being brought to the elder in his or her home. At nutrition sites, other kinds of educational programs can be offered that supplement the food itself; usually participatory programs are the most successful. In addition, the socializing that occurs over the meal can be informational in nature, supplementing the usual lines of communication that the aging may have lost due to changing life conditions. But the delivery program also has success, because the person delivering the food becomes a friendly and anticipated face each day, and the elder can be observed for illness or other need. (Frequently volunteers, themselves aging, may deliver the food.)

**Senior Centers**

These multipurpose gathering points for elders have been viewed by service providers in agencies on aging as one of the most important means of providing information (as well as other services) to the older individual.[26] Perceived as a community focal point, it is difficult to gauge how well received these centers have been by aging people. Perceptions vary widely, and studies have been inconclusive, with findings that appear paradoxical when viewed as a whole. For example, an early study found that individuals under sixty-five who did not use centers tended to be better educated and more affluent than those who did; but the reverse was found for individuals over sixty-five.[27] Studies that attempted to categorize individuals who use the centers as "joiners" or "nonjoiners" have been similarly inconclusive.

The largest mandate for senior centers came in the 1978 amendments to OAA legislation; these amendments provided for center construction as well as the support of services once the centers were opened. Other action has provided some funds for centers through a variety of similar legislation. Most true "centers" provide a combination of activity and service from one location. But some similar organizations are merely "clubs" for elders. In evaluating the types of senior centers, the conclusion must be drawn that they are quite diverse, and programs/services may vary tremendously across the nation, from community to community, and even from site to site within the same community.

Recreation/education and service are the principal distinguishing components of a senior center. As we have noted, the OAA and service providers within it see the centers as particularly good candidates for a focal point to their programs. Because of this, individuals who do not choose to participate in a local center may find that their pipeline to information about aging benefits may be impaired to the point of nonexistence. Public relations for these agencies is extremely expensive, and efforts are not as great as they should be to reach outside the accustomed channels. Senior centers provide an easy way to get the information out, and elders would probably be well advised to maintain some link to a center convenient to them, if they wish to take full advantage of the services and programs available to them by law, especially when administered by the Administration on Aging and its component parts.

### Housing

Ninety-five percent of individuals age sixty-five and older live outside institutional settings. Within this oft-cited figure, though, depending on health and age range, the opportunities for living arrangements are quite diverse. The following categories are provided by Gelfand.[28] Congregate, or sheltered, housing attempts to provide some degree of support to the elderly who are in failing health; frequently one joins such a facility when in relatively good health, with the understanding that if health declines, he or she will be cared for according to need. Foster care is available for individuals who need care, but desire to continue living in a traditional setting; usually the family setting in such arrangements limits the number of elders living together to four. Single-room occupancy hotels are available in cities, and the individuals who choose this type of housing are likely to have worked rather than received assistance in their lifespan, but to have been somewhat alone throughout and perhaps to have received institutional care at some point (mental or penal). Retirement communities are among the most popular options, particularly for the well-to-do. Individuals generally must be older to live there, and no family members who are under eighteen are generally eligible for permanent residency. Shared or accessory housing is becoming, at this writing, more and more popular. An elderly person opens his or her house to a young couple who agree to handle many of the housekeeping tasks in exchange for little or no rent.

The setting in which an elder resides is a major determiner in how that elder's informational needs will be met. Will he or she depend only on an adult child who stops by with groceries and attends to other needs? Or will he or she live in a thriving retirement community, where socializing with bright and motivated people keeps his or her own informational-gathering mode in fine shape? The variations on these two opposite poles are numerous.

### In-home Services

This is a fast-growing segment of care for the elderly, but the need (and the demand) still outstrips the supply. The basic problem is the method of financing such care. Although less expensive than the alternative (institutionalization), and far less traumatic to the elder than an uprooting that is usually unnecessary, governmental agencies have not been funded appropriately to allow such services to proliferate. This is changing, though, and none too soon.

Levels of care can be defined in terms of maximal, intermediate, and limited. (Gelfand calls these categories "intensive or skilled services," "personal care or intermediate services," and "homemaker-chore or basic services."[29] The maximal care requires a complex coordination of highly skilled care, and may be equivalent, though less costly, to the care provided by a nursing home. The intermediate level recognizes a need on the part of aging clients to have certain personal care provided, such as help with bathing and taking medications. Limited, or minimal, care is largely a matter of home maintenance—the supplying of meals, grocery shopping, laundry chores, etc. These various levels of care are provided by health and welfare agencies, in the main. Funding is provided by several governmental sources (particularly Medicare and Medicaid), but also including personal funding by the aging client. The case-management approach has been used to benefit in managing these in-home services for the elderly; however, when caseloads are high (as is common in provider networks), problems mount up and the elderly suffer needlessly.

**Adult Daycare**

A principal hindrance to the ready acceptance of this concept is our society's use of the term, "daycare," for children. In fact, the provision of "daycare" service for adults should be predicated on allowing the individual to contribute meaningfully to his or her care; we are not "molding" an individual by acculturation, as is the case with daycare for children. Perhaps some other way of referring to day-long care programs would allow this very needed program to be better accepted. In today's world, it is likely that the elderly person using daycare cannot be left alone, and is living with adult children who work at full-time jobs. The remainder of the care for the elderly person, in the evenings and on the weekends, is provided by these working adults. Certainly it is no easy task to provide for the needs of one who has ceased to function well on his or her own, and we need to do all that we can to make the situation optimal for both the aging person and his or her children. The older adult is likely also to have great stress in adjusting to declining health and to the life situations of his or her children, who now are, in effect, caretakers of their parent. The emotional pain involved in this altered life status is often greater than the physical limitations might warrant. The habits of a lifetime, in which the elder cared for his or her "young," must be adjusted to fit adult children who are struggling to fulfill many different and new roles themselves.

The range of services provided by daycare is quite broad: medical and nursing care; occupational, physical, and recreational therapy; social work; transportation; meals; personal care; educational programs and crafts; and counseling. To this we must add informational transfer, a function that is so all-pervasive as to be assumed. To handle such a complex array, the client-to-provider ratio must be kept quite low, a factor that makes these programs expensive. Usually adult children have to assume part of the financial burden. In today's society, this solution is difficult at best, but it may be a legitimate choice for individuals who feel strongly that their relative is too healthy for institutionalization, or they feel strongly that institutionalization is wrong (for whatever reasons). The needs of aging clients in this setting are generally great.

**Long-term Care Residences**

This category represents one of the most dreaded and feared outcomes for the elderly at the conclusion of their lives—residence in a nursing home. Although at any one time, only 4–5 percent of the elderly are residing in nursing homes, the percentage increases dramatically with age, and it is this realization that haunts individuals who fear giving up their autonomy and being "put in a home." It is true that most residents have no living spouse, and many have no close relatives at all. Older adults who have a strong support system in place, therefore, are far less likely to have to spend the last years of their lives in a congregate home.

Is it as bad as people fear? There are, in truth, great variations. If the home is chosen carefully, based on enough information about the home's track record, there is less to fear. Usually the elder cannot do this for himself or herself, and family members must be called upon to make these crucial decisions. They need to have the information available to make an informed decision. The for-profit sector is predominant, and regulations must be in place and enforced to ensure that money-making reasons do not compromise the care. Individuals who are more assertive in their rights may fare better in a nursing home; they will speak up if they feel poorly treated, and the complaints will receive attention. In this situation, demanding informational input becomes an adaptive mode. But in any group living situation, personal desire must be, in part, surrendered for the harmonious living of everyone. Having little autonomy in daily decision-making is one of the worst parts of nursing-home living, and as this is recognized and redressed, the situation seems to improve. If elders are given some options in their choice of daily activities, therefore, their morale improves and satisfaction with nursing-home living conditions improve. Informational feedback from the elder thus becomes crucial.

Probably the worst adjustment is in having to change one's environment at the conclusion of one's life. People may have adjusted more readily in earlier years, but as one ages, he or she likes to be surrounded by familiar scenes and fond memories. Much of this is torn asunder when one must enter a nursing home. Supportive family can ease the transition, but the hard truth is that this is one of the most upsetting and potentially life-threatening transitions that anyone ever faces.

### *Summary*

Through the governmental hierarchy for aging services, we have seen a variety of programs and services that have come into their own only in very recent years. We have taken an overview of information-and-referral (the most important program to consider, given our emphasis); health and mental health; transportation; crime and legal assistance; employment and volunteer work; nutrition; senior centers; adult daycare; and long-term care residences. Getting enough information about available programs and services is often the major hurdle in taking advantage of what is, in fact, available. Until the need becomes crucial, most elders do not seek such information because governmental programs have a reputation of being for the "needy," of being "welfare." The attitude in other countries that are more socialized is not so negative, but the independent spirit of Americans has always served to hinder seeking information and help of others unless there is no alternative. Although we may not favor a socialized system, such as in northern Europe, we nevertheless could learn something about the advantage of depending upon others when it is appropriate, *before* one has reached the mental and physical "last resort." Problem-solving, and information about what will solve the problem, can be had at less emotional cost to the elderly person who needs assistance and less turmoil for the supportive family member who seeks to help out.

## Conclusion

Institutional transfer of information is thus pervasive in our society, due in large part to the complexity of our lives. We have observed the influence of the church/synagogue, educational institutions, the library, and governmentally sponsored programs. If we have left the impression that the sources of information are potentially great, that is a true observation—and one we should underscore. In our society, institutions are complex agents for informational transfer to elders. Whether or not they handle the task well is another question. Certainly the potential is there for a vast *number* of ways of transferring information. Research has suggested that the mix of transfer mechanisms *should* be great, because elders themselves are quite diverse and no single way or group of ways can accommodate their needs. This is the great challenge to institutions regarding informational needs today: get out the word (whatever that might be) in as diverse pathways as possible. And *be there* for elders when they have a problem, which is at base a need for information on how to solve that problem.

## Notes

1. Gerhard Wehr, *Jung: A Biography*, trans. David M. Weeks (Boston: Shambhala, 1987), 292, citing C. G. Jung, "Psychotherapie und Seelsorge," in *Die Gesammelten Werke von C. G. Jung* (Zurich: Rascher, 1958–70), 362.
2. Robert M. Gray and David O. Moberg, *The Church and the Older Person* (Grand Rapids, Mich.: Eerdmans, 1977), 85, reporting David O. Moberg, "Christian Beliefs and Personal Adjustment in Old Age," *Journal of the American Scientific Affiliation* 10 (March 1958): 8–12.
3. Celia Elaine Hales, "Planning for the Information Needs of the Aging: A Delphi Study" (Ph.D. diss., Florida State University, 1982), 227.
4. Celia Hales, *How Should the Information Needs of the Aging Be Met?* (Minneapolis: University of Minnnesota Libraries, ERIC Document Reproduction Service No. 294 582, 1987).
5. Louis Lowy and Darlene O'Connor, *Why Education in the Later Years?* (Lexington, Mass.: Lexington Books, 1986), xv.
6. Ibid., 64–65, citing Patricia K. Cross, "Adult Learners: Characteristics, Needs, and Interests," in *Lifelong Learning in America*, ed. Richard E. Peterson and Associates (San Francisco: Jossey-Bass, 1979), 75.
7. John W. C. Johnstone and Ramon J. Rivera, *Volunteers for Learning: A Study of the Educational Pursuits of American Adults* (Chicago: Aldine, 1965).
8. Robert R. Carkhuff, *The Art of Helping: An Introduction to Life Skills* (Amherst, Mass.: Human Resource Development Press, 1973); and Charles B. Truax and

Robert R. Carkhuff, *Toward Effective Counseling and Psychotherapy: Training and Practice* (Chicago: Aldine, 1967).

9. Howard Y. McClusky, "Education for Aging: The Scope of the Field and Perspectives for the Future," in *Learning for Aging*, ed. Stanley M. Grabowski and W. Dean Mason (Washington, D.C.: Adult Education Association, 1974), 324–55.
10. "Guidelines for Library Service to Older Adults," *RQ* 26 (Summer 1987): 444–47.
11. Kenneth Ferstl, "Public Librarians and Service to the Aging: A Study of Attitudes" (Ph.D. diss., Indiana University, 1977), 1.
12. Hales, "Planning for the Information Needs of the Aging."
13. Ibid., 204.
14. Elizabeth D. Huttman, *Social Services for the Elderly* (New York: Free Press, 1985), 52.
15. Donald E. Gelfand, *The Aging Network: Programs and Services* (New York: Springer, 1988), 65.
16. Huttman, *Social Services for the Elderly*, 61, reporting Anita Harbert and Leon Ginsberg, eds., *Human Services for Older Adults: Concepts and Skills* (Belmont, Calif.: Wadsworth, 1979).
17. Ibid., 60.
18. Ibid.
19. Celia Hales, unpublished data, 1980.
20. Mark Battle & Associates, *Evaluation and Referral Services for the Elderly* (Washington, D.C.: Government Printing Office, 1977).
21. Gelfand, *The Aging Network*.
22. Hales, "Planning for the Information Needs of the Aging," 204.
23. Hales, *How Should the Information Needs of the Aging Be Met?*
24. Gelfand, *The Aging Network*, 103.
25. Ibid., 136.
26. Hales, "Planning for the Information Needs of the Aging," 222.
27. Joyce Leanse and Sara B. Wagner, *Senior Centers: A Report of Senior Group Programs in America* (Washington, D.C.: National Council on the Aging, 1975).
28. Gelfand, *The Aging Network*, 176–85.
29. Ibid., 190–91.

# PART IV

# SERVING OLDER ADULTS WITH SPECIAL NEEDS

Throughout our discussion thus far, we have dealt with mainstream elders—those in whom the aging process can be called "normal," and who have enjoyed the fruits of the best that America can offer in a given lifespan. We know, of course, that this is a kind of benign fiction, in that elders are a highly diverse group of people, and sometimes the problems (informational as well as other) may be greater than the norm. In looking at characteristics that distinguish some elders from others, we will study two groups as distinct entities (although it will be obvious that the two converge for a small minority of elder individuals, and this combination of age, gender, and race vulnerability is quite significant).[1] We will examine first the elderly with major health problems, who are vulnerable largely for medical reasons; most older adults in this group constitute the "oldest-old" of the elderly population, and they are disproportionately women (and frequently widowed, a corollary of the fact that women are more likely to outlive their husbands). Then we will examine the current situation of aging ethnic minorities in the United States. Many from this group have not always been able to live the American dream, and the problems of aging are likely to be greater because of the discrimination to which they have been subjected over their lifespan. These two subsets of the aging are not the only ones that differ from the norm, of course, but they are arguably the most important variations that need special examination.

## Note

1. Robert C. Atchley, "Defining the Vulnerable Older Population," in *The Vulnerable Aged: People, Services, and Policies*, ed. Zev Harel, Phyllis Ehrlich, and Richard Hubbard (New York: Springer, 1990), 19.

CHAPTER

# 9

# Serving the Aging with Major Health Problems

Harel, Ehrlich, and Hubbard edited in 1990 an important book for examining vulnerability in the aging, entitled, appropriately enough, *The Vulnerable Aged: People, Services, and Policies.*[1] A wide array of gerontologists and other professionals knowledgeable about the aging process penned essays that spanned the range of issues that will concern us here. Accordingly, much of our analysis will be based upon the arguments set forth in this volume. Its definition of "vulnerability," however, is slightly different from what we wish to describe in analyzing disabilities among the aging. The elder, in our definition of having "major health problems," indicates that the aging process, rather than being considered "normal," has deteriorated into the abnormal; conditions exist that are not endemic to aging, and are real risks to the continued autonomous living of the elder. (Indeed, individuals of any age can and do have major health problems, but the aging are more likely to be so identified.) These are the same people who are sometimes characterized in the literature as the "frail elderly." The oldest-old need assistance in a variety of ways. Their ages tend to be eighty and older, and, as time goes by, the age at which one becomes classified as among the oldest-old tends to get higher due to the better health of the elderly in the United States today. Obviously, the older a person is, the more likely that he or she will fall into this category. Moreover, it is likely that the health condition that labels a person "disabled" will be chronic rather than acute, and multiple conditions of ill health can be the norm.[2] The treatment is therefore altered in sometimes startling ways from the treatment afforded a younger person. And this, in itself, can sometimes be cause for concern. Consequently, although Harel, Ehrlich, and Hubbard and their contributing authors look at a variety of factors that can contribute to vulnerability, we will limit our analysis to the more common problem of declining health toward the extreme end of the continuum. By way of proving their vulnerability, let us cite the statistic that although the aged constitute only a little more than 10 percent of the general population, they accounted for over 30 percent of the money spent for health care in the 1970s and 1980s.[3] While elders may fear other reasons for becoming "vulnerable," these other reasons are not as germane to aging as is the problem of a precipitating crisis in well-being, followed by a long period of adjustment to ill health—with little or no hope for a better life.

Our analysis has heretofore been consistently upbeat, but we would do a disservice to our readers if we did not acknowledge that there is, recognizably, a "dark side" to aging. This dark side is a fearful picture that so many younger people and elders themselves look to with dread. The stereotype would say that most elders are in or close to a disabled state; we have seen that this is not true, but we must look at the situation of a minority of elders for whom this fact is a reality. Keep in mind, though, that we will provide directions for alleviating some of the misery. And we will continue to stress the gathering of information as a necessary and important part of a problem-solving approach. We will see that even a person in pain and close to death does not always have to experience extreme distress—especially psychological—if the right combination of supportive people and institutional structures are in place. And we will identify what some of those people and support structures should do for elders with severe health problems.

## Identifying Elders Who Are Disabled

Two highly technical classifications are used for assessing the degree to which aging people are capable of handling their everyday needs with respect to their overall health condition. The degree to which one can carry out basic activities of daily living—bathing, dressing, grooming, eating by oneself, sometimes mobility, etc.—is termed the degree of "activities of daily living" (ADL) that one has. Activities such as housework, perhaps driving a car, etc., are termed "instrumental activities of daily living" (IADL). The statistics of these figures are reassuring, however—if statistics themselves are considered. At age seventy-five, only 7 percent of older people (men and women) have two or more ADL impairments. Although by age ninety, this figure rises to 18 percent for men and 27 percent for women, it is clearly still a minority. Only 12 percent of those eighty-five and older were found unable to carry out the usual activities of everyday life.[4] These figures, however, do indicate that the oldest individuals are the ones with the greatest health problems—a fact that is well recognized in everyday society.[5] Atchley concludes that about 7 percent of all older adults are in the "frail category" and about 11 percent are immediately at risk—a minority, but one that we should examine closely for need.[6]

## Getting Information as a Way to Cope

Obviously the time for support systems is at hand when an individual lacks the ability to handle the everyday task of living. Knowing what to do—and how to do it—is a major predicament for the adult children of these aging people. The fact that an emotional element is present often complicates the situation immeasurably. Emotional conflicts from childhood may come into the picture for the first time in years—conflicts that the adult child thought, erroneously, had already been worked through. The elder may not take kindly to being assisted, particularly when the one offering assistance is the child whom he or she once nurtured. As has often been cited in the popular press, the turnabout of roles is a crucial one. The adult child may find it very difficult to see his or her parent in declining health; not only is the parent's mortality at risk, but the adult child sees his or her own future predicted, perhaps, because of genetic predisposition.

The best system of supports will fail unless one knows where to turn for assistance. This is the informational aspect so often stressed in this book. In fact, the degree to which an adult child seeks information to alleviate this problem varies tremendously among people. One may take full advantage of the aging hierarchy of agencies, information and referral, and the social service system (when necessary). Another may rely solely on the advice of a trusted physician. In any of these scenarios, the presence of sufficient information to get a good grip on solving the problem is imperative. It can sound naive to say that the more information one gleans, the more likely one is to solve the problem. One may hit upon a solution by simply going to the right person first. But this is unlikely. By and large, the more one learns about the aging process as it relates to a beloved elder, the better able one is to assist that elder in need. By and large, phone calls and visits need to be made as the need is first recognized. The truth is that the answers will vary as increasing degrees of disability arise, and the more one learns at the outset about the possibilities, the better able the adult child can cope.

Certainly it is important to talk to the physician (and possibly the family lawyer as well, as financial repercussions are endemic to that situation), but there are also many, many social agencies that can help. A call to the local aging information-and-referral service may be the gateway to a vast array of services available, services that would go untapped unless that first phone call were made. More and more services are available now that allow an elderly person who needs assistance to remain nevertheless in his or her home. With a little help from the outside, this becomes the solution of choice very, very frequently. Disruption of daily routine is kept to a minimum, and the aging person is not required to tear up longstanding relationships in the neighborhood, nor displace familiar and treasured objects in the home.

The better off the aging person is financially, the less "at risk" he or she is, statistically.[7] Having sufficient income serves as a buffer against vulnerability. Of course, these statistics can be turned on their side to assert that it is the health ailment that precedes vulnerability, that paying the medical costs makes one vulnerable, financially as well as in other, less tangible ways. Given our society, this is an obvious scenario; health care costs are skyrocketing, and affordable health insurance is not yet in sight for many individuals. It is likely that the better insurance policies were left behind at the time of retirement, and the elder may have succumbed to unethical practices in the insurance industry that amounted to scams—health insurance that does not pay at all, or pays so little as to be negligible at the time of need. Obviously, this is one time that obtaining further information was a crying need.

One positive aspect in regard to coping in general is that it tends not to be correlated with age *per se*.[8] There *is* a correlation between "active" and "passive" coping, related to age, in that the older a person is, the more passive he or she may be in regard to seeking help. Older individuals tend to seek out further information less readily than their younger counterparts, and they may not focus on solving the problem itself as a way of obtaining relief.[9] Part of the skill retained in coping, however, may be related to the oft-cited characteristic of women being more assertive when they are older than when they were younger. Because women make up such a large part of the oldest-old population, this characteristic becomes a strong identifying marker for the population itself. Obviously, there is some paradox in these findings; the more assertive that one is, the more likely it would appear that he or she would actively reach out, in a problem-solving mode, for solutions to problems. More research is needed to determine the source of this seeming conflict.

The oldest individuals do not appear to use escape mechanisms in coping nearly as often as their younger counterparts do. Kahana, Kahana, and Kinney say that four times as many young-old people use eating, drinking, smoking, etc., as coping mechanisms in stress than the oldest-old.[10] This would appear to be a positive statement about the oldest-old. Surely, all things being equal, one should choose less escapist tactics to handle problems.

If stress follows on stress, though, the oldest-old are at a disadvantage; they appear less able to rebound and to go on with life at a more normal pace. This is a self-evident conclusion that even most laypeople would recognize as a characteristic of the toll that age takes on individuals.

The most frequently cited way to cope is to seek more information about the difficulty, and then take definite action that seeks to alleviate the distress. This, of course, falls right in line with the major thesis of this book.

## Assisting with Extreme Distress

It is often true that no one knows what another is going through if he or she has never experienced it. This is *a priori* fact when dealing with the oldest-old who have sustained severe health crises. It is useful to acknowledge ignorance in such a case. An older individual *knows* that any other person, however well meaning, is actually outside of the problem, and may resent the appearance of understanding that actually borders on patronization. Of course, to express ignorance goes against the grain for many professionals. But it also may be the older individual who is the professional in regard to his or her own *life*. Listen to what that person says. The clues gained from this simple practice may open up new avenues for treatment, especially psychological. An empathetic heart is sometimes, in reality, all that professionals can offer.

It is wise that professionals never get carried away with sustaining life—or, more exactly, prolonging death—when the oldest-old individual is near death. The proliferation of living wills attests to the difficulties that our society is having with the problem of increased technological support in cases of medical extremes; i.e., individuals actually near death. The fact that many individuals have opted to write such living wills is a testament to the fact that, by and large, a great many people do not want to be kept "living" artificially. Every effort should be made to determine the wishes of the dying person while he or she is still conscious and able to make decisions without coercion. Sometimes family members are loath to "give up" a member, and they may, in fact, insist that heroic measures be carried out—despite (if there is no legal document) the expressed wishes of the individual near death. There are no easy answers, because every case is different. But having a living will remains, in today's climate, the best assurance that one's wishes in regard to medical treatment will be honored at the end.

## Summary

So we do see, as we have known all along, that individuals do eventually approach death, and all of the positive statistics in the world do not change this stark fact. In today's secular world, fewer individuals are able to sustain relief at this ultimate conclusion to life on earth by religious means. Consequently, in our technological world, we have "given up" on some types of information that, for earlier generations, were highly meaningful and ultimately made the whole experience easier to accept—not only for the older individual who was dying, but for his or her family and friends as well. The fact does remain, though, that the end is not distressingly painful for the vast majority; it is the minority who suffer greatly who have made the specter of death so frightful for so many. Ultimately, no book can give answers to such questions. They must be found within the inner resources of the individual—whether one calls this "God," or "Fate," or the "Unknown." People who are trying to help would do well to acknowledge their limitations; there are, after all, some mysteries of life and death in whose presence even the greatest earthly physicians are quiet.

## Notes

1. Zev Harel, Phyllis Ehrlich, and Richard Hubbard, eds., *The Vulnerable Aged: People, Services, and Policies* (New York: Springer, 1990).

2. Aloen Townsend and Zev Harel, "Health Vulnerability and Service Need among the Aged," in Harel, Ehrlich, and Hubbard, eds., *The Vulnerable Aged,* 34.
3. Ibid., 32, citing National Council on Aging, *Fact Book on Aging* (Washington, D.C.: National Council on Aging, 1978); and Fredric D. Wolinsky, Rodney M. Coe, and Ray R. Mosely, "The Use of Health Services by Elderly Americans: Implications from a Regression-Based Cohort Analysis," in *Health in Aging: Sociological Issues and Policy Directions*, ed. Russell A. Ward and Sheldon S. Tobin (New York: Springer, 1987), 106–32.
4. M. G. Kovar, "Aging in the Eighties: Preliminary Data from the Supplement on Aging to the National Health Interview Survey, United States, January–June 1984," *Advance Data from Vital & Health Statistics* (No. 115, DHHS Publication No. PHS 866–1250) (Hyattsville, Md.: U.S. Public Health Service, May 1, 1986).
5. S. R. Kunkel and R. A. Applebaum, "The Future of Long-Term Care: Projections and Challenges," Paper presented at the annual meeting of the Gerontological Society of America, San Francisco, November 1988, reported by Robert C. Atchley, "Defining the Vulnerable Older Population," in Harel, Ehrlich, and Hubbard, eds., *The Vulnerable Aged,* 22.
6. Atchley, "Defining the Vulnerable Older Population," 30.
7. Ronald L. Simons and Gale E. West, "Life Changes, Coping Resources, and Health among the Elderly," *International Journal on Aging and Human Development* 20 (1985): 1984–85, reported by Eva Kahana, Boza Kahana, and Jennifer Kinney, "Coping among Vulnerable Elders," in Harel, Ehrlich, and Hubbard, eds., *The Vulnerable Aged,* 70.
8. Robert R. MacCrae, "Age Difference in the Use of Coping Mechanisms," *Journal of Gerontology* 37 (July 1982): 454–60.
9. Carolyn M. Aldwin and Tracey A. Revenson, "Does Coping Help? A Reexamination of the Relation between Coping and Mental Health," *Journal of Personality and Social Psychology* 53 (August 1987): 77.
10. Kahana, Kahana, and Kinney, "Coping among Vulnerable Elders," 79.

# CHAPTER 10

# Serving the Aging Who Are Ethnic Minorities

The older adult who is an ethnic minority is doubly discriminated against in our society; not only is aging itself frequently treated with disrespect because of the American love affair with youth, but the ethnic minority elder (if he or she is not first generation) is culminating a lifetime of discrimination that will influence the degree of economic and sometimes social support that he or she has in the twilight years. We will study the groups of elderly who are most highly represented statistically in the population: African-Americans, Hispanic-Americans, and Asian-Americans. To some extent the discussion can be extrapolated to include Native Americans as well as other, smaller groups, but this must be done with caution. Ethnic minorities are quite diverse, and so judgments about one that are generalized to others usually do not work; moreover, very few studies and virtually no reviews exist of minorities that are smaller than the three that we will discuss. And only in the last five years have studies of even these three become numerous. Our society is just catching up with the great need to provide for *all* of its members. Let us take a look at the role of information as it relates specifically to the more numerous ethnic minorities in the United States. We will first identify certain variables common to all groups, and then discuss the groups in order of their numbers (greatest to smallest percentage of the U.S. population).

## Utilizing Social Services Available to Elders

An outstanding assessment of this important variable is made by Markides and Mindel.[1] They note that in this matter ethnicity seems to make little difference in the *categories* of reasons that predict use of social agencies and their programs; the same predicting factors that account for the majority of American elderly also predict for elderly minorities.

One of the most important variables, if not *the* most important, is the degree of closeness that an elder has with family—children or extended family, including siblings. If the closeness is great, elders will not take advantage of social (largely governmental) support nearly as often. Markides and Mindel point to a problem that is potentially discriminatory in regard to the delivery of social services: Because ethnic minorities are typically believed to "take care of their own," the governmental hierarchy may neglect to reach out sufficiently, creating de facto discriminative distribution of services. Gallego goes so far as to suggest that this cultural myth offers an excuse to the establishment not to reach out sufficiently to minorities.[2]

For our purposes, though, we do not need to explore in depth this controversial issue, but simply need to note that the degree to which familial closeness exists is very, very likely to predict the kinds and amount of information that elders will receive in solving their problems. If that part of the family still quite active in society and cognizant of its changes is "on call" to assist the needy elder, the elder is more likely to learn of ways to solve problems by gathering the information necessary to do just that. Markides and Mindel state the issue succinctly: "It has been found that the informal support system, particularly the family, has been an important source of information regarding availability of formally provided social services and health care services."[3] Cicirelli makes the even more cogent point that the family will often "act as an information and referral source."[4] Specifically, in regard to one group—African-Americans—Mindel and Wright found that the more closely linked the family was to the elderly person, the more likely the elder was to use the services of the aging network; one source of support was therefore seen as complementary to and not supplanting the other.[5] This is in direct opposition to the prevailing cultural myth, discussed above.

A significant barrier to utilization of social service agencies, such as the aging network, though, is the fact that the *uniqueness* of the ethnic minority has not been taken into account. One obvious example is the fact of a potential language barrier in the case of Hispanic-Americans or Asian-Americans. Because many of the staff working with the elderly are of the ethnic majority, it may be difficult to "walk in the shoes" of all elderly people, and so their own participation in the planning of programs is vital. This is an idea that is very prevalent in regard to all types of programs for the elderly, and when working with minorities, it is particularly relevant. The bureaucracy is likely to be a real turnoff for minority elderly; the rules by which interactions are made may not "work" with ethnic minorities. For example, many elderly people, whether minorities or not, do not wish to answer personal questions when they do not know or trust the questioner. But the staff member may believe that getting these answers is crucial to developing a successful program. And so a kind of stalemate develops; the aging person does not cooperate (in the view of the staff member), and so the program never really gets off the ground. This makes for discrimination, built frequently upon misunderstanding of cultural differences.

Carole Cox makes this point comprehensively.[6] She cites Harbert and Ginsberg as making the point that language barriers and programs insensitive to cultural traditions and beliefs are two of the most fundamental problems in planning aging services for ethnic minorities.[7] Without staff members having had sufficient education to see beyond these barriers, and compounded by the presumed belief that families will take care of minorities, the stage is set for underutilization of the social programs for the aging, and real discrimination in the delivery of services meant for all elders in our society. Minority elders may be suspicious of the help as well, having known discrimination in their lives previously, and this will unwittingly undermine the aging agency's attempts to assist.

## Serving African-American Older Adults

African-American older adults have experienced the discrimination that we noted earlier to a far greater extent than any other minority group in our history. The older adult today is likely to be the grandchild or great-grandchild of slaves; this commonality in background suggests the ambivalence about the African-American elder that our society still displays. In no other group has it been felt so keenly that a group would "take care of its own." The important place of the church in the lives of many black elderly has seemed, unfortunately, to be justification that social agencies *not* reach out aggressively to solve problems of this group. The church, being present and wanting to care for those in obvious need, has in fact assisted immeasurably, but there is no indication that it has been able to do so in a more efficacious manner than society as a whole could have done. It has been the default mechanism, not unlike those black institutions in general that assisted the black elderly when the larger society failed to respond.

The church, in fact, assists after the older individual has first turned to the wider kinship-and-friends network.[8] African-American elders look first to their children (if the spouse is dead); there is evidence that this group has greater expectations of being cared for by their children than people in general, especially whites. From that initial seeking, the individual may reach further outward—to siblings, cousins, "adopted" kin, and friends. Only after these avenues have been tapped does a black elder then turn to his or her church. There is, of course, much overlap, because many of these same people will be members of the same congregation.

What does this pattern postulate about informational transfer? Obviously, the more knowledgeable these individuals are about sources of support (financial and otherwise) and other problems dependent upon information to solve, the more likely that a black elder will live more comfortably in his or her final years. It suggests as well that we should make sure that we target the black population in general, with information designed to assist the black elder; the mediating influence of other, younger people is particularly evident with black society, and, because of this, we will be far more successful in reaching out to them if we make sure that younger people (and older) are in our communication network. What does not work so well is to assume that white people, or indeed people of any ethnic background other than black, will solve the problem of a lack of information very fundamentally. African-Americans look to their own race, frequently, for solutions to problems; this is surely due not merely to convenience, but also to the fact of being disappointed by the larger society so many times. Taylor and Chatters make this point comprehensively and knowledgeably in regard to family, friends, and the church support network.[9] They write with an appreciative tone of what this system, parallel to society's at large, has achieved.

There is evidence that the older black individual may not fear old age as much as others in society do. Because frequently he or she has been forced to work at menial jobs for a living, there will be great anticipation and expectation of retirement. It becomes something to be welcomed, rather than the end of challenge as understood and experienced by the white majority, particularly the male majority. Jackson and Gibson note that the retirement years, indeed, may be among the happiest of a lifetime.[10] This optimistic slant to the older years is particularly welcome, given the negatives of discrimination to which the individual has been forced to accommodate throughout his or her lifetime.

## Serving Hispanic-American Older Adults

Hispanic-American older adults are frequently poorly understood by staff who work in aging programs. There are a variety of reasons for this, many of which are culturally determined. First, and most important, there is likely to be a language barrier. This is a fundamental reason why informational transfer does not occur, or occurs with misunderstanding and confusion about the motives of one person to another. Unfortunately, when the Older Americans Act was being prepared, research uncovered that very few staff members who work with the aging have any bilingual skills. And many older Hispanic-Americans do not speak English.[11] Second, there are often cultural differences between the staff member and the older Hispanic that are not easily overcome; their expectations are different. Specifically, staff members frequently expect great self-disclosure in interviews; they wish for the older person to share easily and completely the problems of living that are confronting him or her.[12] But Hispanic elderly do not share easily with people who are strangers; they want, reasonably enough, to get to know and trust the person, to make of him or her a friend, before revealing intimate details of their lives. In this matter of sharing, in fact, Hispanic-American elderly are only different in degree from the majority of elderly, who frequently object to the intrusion of strangers in what they rightly recognize to be family matters (and believe should remain private).

Staff workers not only must overcome this resistance, but they also must learn more about the structure of the Hispanic elder's family, which is likely to be a pattern of extended interaction in the various affairs of living. Hispanic elders have consistently higher levels of interaction with their children and grandchildren than the majority of elders in the United States.[13] Hispanic-American elderly are more likely to relate intergenerationally, and the majority of elders are more likely to interact with siblings and friends. Indeed, the older Hispanic enjoys a status that the majority of older adults do not: status as an elder and recognition of his or her contribution to the larger family, especially in the rearing of children.[14] Because of this pattern of interaction, it is possible that many needs of this group will be solved by someone in the extended family. Using the model that we have been developing, we recognize that the more diverse one's sources of support, the more likely that the information needed to solve problems will be forthcoming. If one individual does not have the wherewithal to solve the problem (or know where to go for information that will assist in the solution), another can be found who does.

Support for the above conclusion is available from a comprehensive study carried out by Starrett and Decker among Mexican-American elderly.[15] They evaluated 1,805 randomly selected, noninstitutionalized elderly Hispanics. They studied "enabling variables," i.e., those factors that would predispose an elderly Mexican-American to seek assistance with problems within the aging network. Some 36 variables in all were checked. Significantly, only *two* factors were found to directly influence the extent to which Hispanic elderly used the aging network: (1) knowledge of social services and (2) family income. The specific finding was that if a Hispanic elder knew of the service, and his or her income was low, then he or she was far more likely to take advantage of the offering. For our purposes, though, several other factors were important to the *knowledge* of (i.e., information about) the service: respondents were more aware if they lived alone or only with a spouse (presumably because they had not been able to depend upon others in a close-knit family); if they participated in senior church activities (which were an information conduit and also legitimized the concept of reaching out to others beyond the family); if they were more mobile (probably because of a greater awareness about society in general); and if they were Mexican-American as opposed to Hispanic-American in general.

There is a problem, alluded to earlier, of treating all Hispanic-Americans as though they are similar to one another.[16] The truth is that there are substantial differences between Mexican-Americans, Puerto Rican-Americans, and Cuban-Americans. Because research among any of these groups has been limited, it is often necessary to assume that the similarities outweigh the differences in any given group, in order to have some research, at least, upon which to base a future program. But we should register caution in treating all Hispanic-Americans as though they were identical.

## Serving Asian-American Older Adults

Jik-Joen Lee wrote a sensitive essay entitled, "Asian American Elderly: A Neglected Minority Group."[17] In the process of researching our study, it became all too apparent that Lee was right: Very little research specific to Asian-American elders has been done. The reporting that is found tends, in many respects, to mirror comments that we have found above in regard to Hispanic-Americans. This seems more due to stereotyping than to genuine similarities: studies about one ethnic minority are inappropriately generalized to another because, superficially, they share certain similarities. Nevertheless, with Lee's essay as a basis, let us take a look at what we found in regard to serving Asian-American older adults in the aging network.

Lee found that Asian-American elders had been neglected by social workers and those others who work with the aging, and structurally had been excluded from those services intended for all American elderly. She cites evidence that in several studies an attempt has been made to "prove" that Asian-Americans prefer not to use formal assistance and would prefer to depend upon the informal assistance of their own ethnic community and family. If this criterion were not discriminatory, it could be well argued that *all* older Americans, including all in the ethnic majority, would prefer this solution. But the fact is that the family *cannot* always "provide for its own," and when this safety net is exhausted, society needs to step in and assist its older members.

Lee gives five reasons for the underutilization of aging programs by Asian-Americans. First, programs may be culturally inappropriate, in that social workers are insensitive and unresponsive to the needs of their Asian-American clientele. This is similar to the problem of informational transfer given above for Hispanic-Americans, in that older people may prefer to "get to know" the staff member before sharing intimate details of daily living and the problems entailed in that. Second, there is a value among Asians to be self-reliant and to have a certain pride in *not* bringing personal problems to a stranger. This directly affects the first reason, of course. Third, the history of discrimination against Asian-Americans may make elders of this group suspicious of the government. The forced quarantine of Japanese-Americans during World War II is a crucial point, and it is this group who are among the elders of our nation. Fourth, organizational barriers may impede the utilization of services; the simple fact of the service being outside the neighborhood of the Asian-American elder may influence use far more than one might readily recognize; this amounts to a form of discrimination. And fifth, there is a recognized prejudice in and of itself: Asian-Americans may be discounted because they do not speak English, or they are from a "caste" of immigrants, or they occupy a lower status in the American hierarchy.

Certainly, Asian-American elderly *are* cared for by their own families whenever possible. But we should never let this fact be a barrier to providing access to governmental services that would enhance their style of living. As part of the "information poor," they are in prime need of further outreach on the part of the aging network. And far more research is needed in order to tailor programs to their needs.

## Conclusion

Just as we have assumed in this book that it is important to understand the uniqueness of elders (as opposed to seeing this segment of the population as simply part of the whole), so too is it important to understand ethnicity as a *defining* characteristic of elderly individuals. Gelfand and Barresi assert that ethnicity is not just a demographic variable, but a determiner of personality and a means of coping in a sometimes-hostile environment.[18] We would be wise to heed their words. Until we try to understand the uniqueness of those elderly who are not in the majority, we are likely to project majority values and proclivities onto them—doing them a real disservice as well as being inherently discriminatory. Greater education and interpersonal sensitivity (which can result from greater education) are the twin components in successfully addressing this problem.

## Notes

1. Kyriakos S. Markides and Charles H. Mindel, *Aging and Ethnicity* (Newbury Park, Calif.: Sage, 1987), 222ff.
2. D. Gallego, "The Mexican American Elderly: Familial and Friendship Support System . . . Fact or Fiction," Paper presented at the annual meeting of the Gerontological Society of America, San Diego, 1980; and Jacqueline Johnson Jackson, *Minorities and Aging* (Belmont, Calif.: Wadsworth, 1980).
3. Markides and Mindel, *Aging and Ethnicity*, 223.
4. Markides and Mindel, *Aging and Ethnicity*, 223, citing Victor G. Cicirelli, *Helping Elderly Parents* (Boston: Auburn House, 1981).
5. Charles H. Mindel and Roosevelt Wright, "The Use of Social Services by Black and White Elderly: The Role of Social Support Systems," *Journal of Gerontological*

*Social Work* 4 (Spring/Summer 1982): 107–26; also Charles H. Mindel, Roosevelt Wright, and Richard A. Starrett, "Informal and Formal Social and Health Service Use by Black and White Elderly: A Comparative Cost Approach," *Gerontologist* 26 (June 1986): 279–85.

6. Carole Cox, "Overcoming Access Problems in Ethnic Communities," in *Ethnic Dimensions of Aging*, ed. Donald E. Gelfand and Charles M. Barresi (New York: Springer, 1987).
7. Anita S. Harbert and Leon H. Ginsberg, *Human Services for Older Adults* (Belmont, Calif.: Wadsworth, 1979).
8. Wilbur H. Watson, "Family Care, Economics, and Health," in *Black Aged: Understanding Diversity and Service Needs*, ed. Zev Harel, Edward A. McKinney, and Michael Williams (Newbury Park, Calif.: Sage, 1990), 51.
9. Robert Joseph Taylor and Linda M. Chatters, "Family, Friend, and Church Support Networks of Black Americans," in *Black Adult Development and Aging*, ed. Reginald L. Jones (Berkeley, Calif.: Cobb & Henry, 1989), 245–72.
10. James S. Jackson and Rose C. Gibson, "Work and Retirement among the Black Elderly," in *Current Perspectives on Aging and the Life Cycle*, vol. 1, ed. Zena Blau (Greenwich, Conn.: JAI Press, 1985), 193–222, cited by Harold R. Johnson, Rose C. Gibson, and Irene Luckey, "Health and Social Characteristics: Implications for Services," in Harel, McKinney, and Williams, eds., *Black Aged*, 73.
11. Alejandro Garcia, "Social Policy and Elderly Hispanic," in *Hispanic Elderly in Transition: Theory, Research, Policy, and Practice*, ed. Steven R. Applewhite (New York: Greenwood Press, 1988), 101.
12. Steven R. Applewhite and John M. Daley, "Cross-Cultural Understanding for Social Work Practice with the Hispanic Elderly," in Applewhite, ed., *Hispanic Elderly in Transition*, 9.
13. James E. Lubben and Rosina M. Becerra, "Social Support among Black, Mexican, and Chinese Elderly," in Gelfand and Barresi, eds., *Ethnic Dimensions of Aging*, 130.
14. Marta Sotomayor and Steven R. Applewhite, "The Hispanic Elderly and the Extended Multigenerational Family," in Applewhite, ed., *Hispanic Elderly in Transition*, 124–25.
15. Richard A. Starrett and James T. Decker, "The Utilization of Social Services by the Mexican-American Elderly," in *Ethnicity and Gerontological Social Work*, ed. Rose Dobrof (New York: Haworth Press, 1987), 95.
16. Garcia, "Social Policy and Elderly Hispanic," 103.
17. Jik-Joen Lee, "Asian American Elderly: A Neglected Minority Group," in Dobrof, ed., *Ethnicity and Gerontological Social Work*, 103–16.
18. Gelfand and Barresi, eds., *Ethnic Dimensions of Aging*, 258.

CHAPTER

# 11

# Conclusion—What Does It All Mean?

Thus we have followed a broadly defined route to understanding the information needs of elders who wish to live successfully in today's complex world. After analyzing demographically just who the elderly are in today's society, we spent three chapters (all of part II) analyzing the distinctive features about the aging that make informational transfer unique to them, i.e., the influence of aging processes on the receipt of information. While physiologically, psychologically, and sociologically there is a challenge ahead for all of us who live to be old, this can be addressed best if one seeks the information needed to make the life choices ahead. We learned that aging in and of itself does not have to be viewed as a negative fact, that it is the pathology of illness that carries the negative connotations about which we hear so much. And it is at an increasingly late age that these physical complications make life difficult for the elderly. Consequently, there is much to celebrate about old age today, and much that is benign to learn about the specific characteristics of normal aging that accompany the gain in years. Woven throughout these chapters was the insight that additional information makes life more manageable, happier, and more successful.

We then launched (in part III) into a widespread analysis of information-seeking patterns of elders in society. First, we looked at various academicians' views of the theoretical foundations for information seeking, and then we studied mass media—the means of transmission of information directly. In the definition of mass media used here, we included books, periodicals, newspapers, television, radio, motion pictures, the telephone (as an electronic means of information sharing), and computer technology (to a limited extent, as elders typically do not very readily take to computers). Second, we studied the small circle of intimates to whom the elder will turn first in time of difficulty: family, friends and neighbors, and professionals who have long assisted them in carrying out the daily functions of life (physician, lawyer, and clergy). Third, we looked at the institutions of society that transmit information: the church, educational institutions, libraries, and the government. These institutions sometimes enter the elder's life when the intimate bonds of family and friends have done all they can do to handle difficulty; this is especially true in regard to governmental intervention via social service entitlements. But there is much that institutions do that is far more positive: elders are attending schools at increasing rates, their visits to the public library almost fit the stereotypical notion of heavy library use by elders, and the church plays an increasingly important role in many elders' lives.

Finally, we analyzed the special needs of particular portions of the elderly populace: aging individuals with major health problems, and ethnic minorities.

I would leave you with the thought that it is not growing older that is the threat; it is growing older without the love and support of a caring world. Surely most of us depend to a great extent upon the close bonds that we form with family and friends, but it is the increasingly fragmented world of the 1990s that is the real culprit as we consider our advancing years. Our society has not viewed older people as the resource for information that they are; other cultures frequently believe in the greater knowledge of the elderly, the experience that living has granted them—and those cultures prove this belief by turning to elders with respect. In the United States, conversely, younger adults even worry about the laugh lines that make wrinkles! Our priorities are awry. As elders in our society exercise greater clout as their numbers increase (a product of aging for the Baby Boom generation), we must take a second look at aging, and turn from the threat that it engenders instinctively in most of us. As we support our elders in both their quest for information and the information they share with us from their long life, we will become stronger ourselves; the bonds of love and caring will have made a circle around us all.

# BIBLIOGRAPHY

*Ageing Populations: The Social Policy Implications*. Paris: Organisation for Economic Co-operation and Development; Washington, D.C.: OECD Publications and Information Centre, distributor, 1988.

Aiken, Lewis R. *Later Life*. Philadelphia: Saunders, 1978.

Aldwin, Carolyn A., and Tracey A. Revenson. "Does Coping Help? A Reexamination of the Relation between Coping and Mental Health." *Journal of Personality and Social Psychology* 53 (August 1987): 337–48.

Anderson, Jr., Banks, and Erdman B. Palmore. "Longitudinal Evaluation of Ocular Function." In *Normal Aging II*, 24–31. Ed. by Erdman Palmore. Durham, N.C.: Duke University Press, 1974.

Anson, Roberto. "Cable Television, Telecommunications, and U.S. Hispanic Elderly." In *Hispanic Elderly in Transition: Theory, Research, Policy, and Practice*, 203–20. Ed. by Steven R. Applewhite. New York: Greenwood Press, 1988.

Applebaum, R. A., Robert C. Atchley, and C. Austin. *PASSPORT: A Program Review*. Oxford, Ohio: Scripps Gerontology Center, 1987.

Applewhite, Steven R., ed. *Hispanic Elderly in Transition: Theory, Research, Policy, and Practice*. New York: Greenwood Press, 1988.

Applewhite, Steven R., and John M. Daley. "Cross-Cultural Understanding for Social Work Practice with the Hispanic Elderly." In *Hispanic Elderly in Transition: Theory, Research, Policy, and Practice*, 3–16. Ed. by Steven R. Applewhite. New York: Greenwood Press, 1988.

Arie, Tom, ed. *Health Care of the Elderly: Essays in Old Age Medicine, Psychiatry, and Services*. Baltimore: Johns Hopkins University Press, 1981.

Atchley, Robert C. "Defining the Vulnerable Older Population." In *The Vulnerable Aged: People, Services, and Policies*, 18–31. Ed. by Zev Harel, Phyllis Ehrlich, and Richard Hubbard. New York: Springer, 1990.

______. *Social Forces and Aging: An Introduction to Social Gerontology*. 4th ed. Belmont, Calif.: Wadsworth, 1985.

______. *The Sociology of Retirement*. Cambridge, Mass.: Schenkman, New York: distributed by Halsted Press, 1976.

Atchley, Robert C., and Sheila J. Miller. "Older People and Their Families." In *Annual Review of Gerontology and Geriatrics*, vol. 1, 337–69. Ed. by Carl Eisdorfer. New York: Springer, 1980.

Baran, Stanley J., Jerilyn S. McIntyre, and Timothy P. Meyer. *Self, Symbols and Society: An Introduction to Mass Communication*. 1st ed. New York: Random House, 1984.

Barresi, Charles M., and Geeta Menon. "Diversity in Black Family Caregiving." In *Black Aged: Understanding Diversity and Service Needs*, 221–35. Ed. by Zev Harel, Edward A. McKinney, and Michael Williams. Newbury Park, Calif.: Sage, 1990.

Barusch, Amanda Smith. *Elder Care: Family Training and Support*. Newbury Park, Calif.: Sage, 1991.

Bass, Scott A., Elizabeth A. Kutza, and Fernando M. Torres-Gil. *Diversity in Aging*. Glenview, Ill.: Scott, Foresman, 1990.

Belsky, Janet. *The Psychology of Aging: Theory, Research, and Practice*. Monterey, Calif.: Brooks/Cole, 1984.

Bengtson, Vern L., and Neal E. Cutler. "Generations and Intergenerational Relations." In *Handbook of Aging and the Social Sciences*, 130–59. Ed. by Robert H. Binstock and Ethel Shanas. New York: Van Nostrand, 1976.

Binstock, Robert H., and Ethel Shanas, eds. *Handbook of Aging and the Social Sciences*. New York: Van Nostrand, 1976.

———. *Handbook of Aging and the Social Sciences*. 2d ed. New York: Van Nostrand, 1985.

Birren, James E. *The Psychology of Aging*. Englewood Cliffs, N.J.: Prentice-Hall, 1964.

Birren, James E., and K. Warner Schaie, eds. *Handbook of the Psychology of Aging*. New York: Van Nostrand, 1977.

———. *Handbook of the Psychology of Aging*. 2nd ed. New York: Van Nostrand, 1985.

Bittner, John R. *Mass Communication: An Introduction*. 4th ed. Englewood Cliffs, N.J.: Prentice-Hall, 1986.

Blau, Zena Smith. *Aging in a Changing Society*. 2d ed. New York: Franklin Watts, 1981.

Blenker, Margaret. "Social Work and Family Relationships in Later Life with Some Thoughts on Filial Maturity." In *Social Structure and the Family*, 46–59. Ed. by Ethel Shanas and Gordon F. Streib. Englewood Cliffs, N.J.: Prentice-Hall, 1965.

Bliese, Nancy Wood. "Media in the Rocking Chair: Media Uses and Functions among the Elderly." In *Inter/Media: Interpersonal Communication in a Media World*, 573–82. Ed. by Gary Gumpert and Robert Cathcart. New York: Oxford University Press, 1986.

Bochner, Arthur P., Edmund P. Kaminski, and Mary Anne Fitzpatrick. "The Conceptual Domain of Interpersonal Communication Behavior: A Factor-Analytic Study." *Human Communication Research* 3 (Summer 1977): 291–302.

Booth, Tim. *Home Truths: Old People's Homes and the Outcome of Care.* Brookfield, Vt.: Gower, 1985.

Bordewich, Fergus M. "Supermarketing the Newspaper." *Columbia Journalism Review* 16 (September/October 1977): 23–30.

Botwinick, Jack. *Aging and Behavior: A Comprehensive Integration of Research Findings.* 2d ed. New York: Springer, 1978.

Botwinick, Jack, and James E. Birren. "Mental Abilities and Psychomotor Responses in Healthy Aged Men." In *Human Aging: A Biological and Behavioral Study,* 97–108. Ed. by James E. Birren et al. Washington, D.C.: U.S. Public Health Service, 1963.

Botwinick, Jack, and Martha Storandt. "Cardiovascular Status, Depressive Affect and Other Factors in Reaction." *Journal of Gerontology* 29 (September 1974): 543–48.

Brearley, C. Paul. *Working in Residential Homes for Elderly People.* London: Tavistock/Routledge, 1990.

Breivik, Patricia Senn, and E. Gordon Gee. *Information Literacy: Revolution in the Library.* New York: American Council on Education, Macmillan, 1989; London: Collier Macmillan, 1989.

Britton, Joseph H., and Jean O. Britton. "The Middle-Aged and Older Rural Person and His Family." In *Older Rural Americans,* 44–74. Ed. by E. Grant Youmans. Lexington: University of Kentucky, 1967.

Browne, Colette, and Roberta Onzuka-Anderson, eds. *Our Aging Parents: A Practical Guide to Eldercare.* Honolulu: University of Hawaii Press, 1985.

Brubaker, Ellie. *Working with the Elderly: A Social Systems Approach.* Newbury Park, Calif.: Sage, 1987.

Bryson, Lyman. *The Communication of Ideas.* New York: Cooper Square, 1948.

Budd, Richard W., and Brent D. Ruben, eds. *Beyond Media: New Approaches to Mass Communication.* Rochelle Park, N.J.: Hayden, 1979.

Butler, Robert N. *Aging and Mental Health: Positive Psychosocial Approaches.* St. Louis: Mosby, 1973.

Butler, Robert N., and Myrna I. Lewis. *Aging and Mental Health: Positive Psychosocial Approaches.* 2d ed. St. Louis: Mosby, 1977.

Carkhuff, Robert R. *The Art of Helping.* 5th ed. Amherst, Mass.: Human Resource Development Press, 1983.

______. *The Art of Helping: An Introduction to Life Skills.* Amherst, Mass.: Human Resource Development Press, 1973.

Carp, Frances M. "Housing and Living Environments of Older People." In *Handbook of Aging and the Social Sciences,* 244–71. Ed. by Robert H. Binstock and Ethel Shanas. New York: Van Nostrand, 1976.

Casey, Genevieve M. *Library Services for the Aging.* Hamden, Conn.: Library Professional, 1984.

Chatters, Linda M., and Robert Joseph Taylor. "Social Integration." In *Black Aged: Understanding Diversity and Service Needs*, 82–99. Ed. by Zev Harel, Edward A. McKinney, and Michael Williams. Newbury Park, Calif.: Sage, 1990.

Cicirelli, Victor G. *Helping Elderly Parents*. Boston: Auburn House, 1981.

Clark, Margaret, and Barbara Gallatin Anderson. *Culture and Aging: An Anthropological Study of Older Americans*. Springfield, Ill.: C. C. Thomas, 1967.

Clements, William M. *Ministry with the Aging*. San Francisco: Harper, 1981.

Congressional Quarterly, Inc. *Aging in America: The Federal Government's Role*. Washington, D.C.: Congressional Quarterly, 1989.

Corey, Gerald. *Issues and Ethics in the Helping Professions*. 3d ed. Pacific Grove, Calif.: Brooks/Cole, 1988.

Cornish, Edward, ed. *Communications Tomorrow: The Coming of the Information Society: Selections from The Futurist*. Bethesda, Md.: World Future Society, 1982.

Corso, John F. *Aging Sensory Systems and Perception*. New York: Praeger, 1981.

Cox, Carole. "Overcoming Access Problems in Ethnic Communities." In *Ethnic Dimensions of Aging*, 165–78. Ed. by Donald E. Gelfand and Charles M. Barresi. New York: Springer, 1987.

Cox, Harold. *Later Life: The Realities of Aging*. Englewood Cliffs, N.J.: Prentice-Hall, 1984.

Craik, F. I. M., and Sandra Trehub, eds. *Aging and Cognitive Processes*. New York: Plenum Press, 1982.

Cross, Patricia K. "Adult Learners: Characteristics, Needs, and Interests." In *Lifelong Learning in America*, 75–141. Ed. by Richard E. Peterson and Associates. San Francisco: Jossey-Bass, 1979.

Davis, Lenwood, comp. *The Black Aged in the United States: A Selectively Annotated Bibliography*. 2d ed. New York: Greenwood Press, 1989.

Davis, Richard H. "Television Communication and the Elderly." In *Aging: Scientific Perspectives and Social Issues*. New York: Van Nostrand, 1975.

De Grazia, Sebastian. "The Uses of Time." In *Aging and Leisure*, 113–54. Ed. by Robert Watson Kleemeier. New York: Oxford University Press, 1961.

De Sola Pool, Ithiel, et al., eds. *Handbook of Communication*. Chicago: Rand McNally, 1973.

Dee, Marianne, and Judith Bowen. *Library Services to Older People*. London: British Library; Dover, N.H.: distributed by Longwood Publishing Group, 1986.

Deichman, Elizabeth S., and Regina Kociecki. *Working with the Elderly*. Buffalo, N.Y.: Prometheus Books, 1989.

Dennis, Wayne. "Age and Achievement: A Critique." *Journal of Gerontology* 11 (April 1956): 331–33.

Dobrof, Rose, ed. *Ethnicity and Gerontological Social Work*. New York: Haworth Press, 1987.

Doughty, Stephen V. *Ministry of Love: A Handbook for Visiting the Aged*. Notre Dame, Ind.: Ave Maria Press, 1984.

Downing, Ruppert A. "Human Services and the Black Adult Life Cycle." In *Black Adult Development and Aging*, 273–96. Ed. by Reginald L. Jones. Berkeley, Calif.: Cobb & Henry, 1989.

Dreher, Barbara Bender. *Communication Skills for Working with Elders*. New York: Springer, 1987.

Driedger, Leo, and Neena Chappell. *Aging and Ethnicity: Toward an Interface*. Toronto: Butterworths, 1987.

Dunkle, Ruth E., Marie R. Haugh, and Marvine Rosenberg, eds. *Communications Technology and the Elderly: Issues and Forecasts*. New York: Springer, 1984.

Dychtwald, Ken. *New Directions for Eldercare Services: Cooperation along the Continuum*. New York: McGraw-Hill Information Services, 1990.

Egan, Gerard. *The Skilled Helper: A Systematic Approach to Effective Helping*. 3d ed. Pacific Grove, Calif.: Brooks/Cole, 1986.

Eisdorfer, Carl, ed. *Review of Gerontology and Geriatrics*. Vol. 1. New York: Springer, 1980.

Emery, Michael, and Ted Curtis Smythe, comps. *Readings in Mass Communication: Concepts and Issues in the Mass Media*. 5th ed. Dubuque, Iowa: W. C. Brown Company, 1983.

Emmert, Phil, and William C. Donaghy. *Human Communication: Elements and Contexts*. Reading, Mass.: Addison-Wesley, 1981.

Epstein, Leon J. "Depression in the Elderly." *Journal of Gerontology* 31 (May 1976): 278–82.

Epstein, Seymour. "The Stability of Behavior: On Predicting Most of the People Much of the Time." *Journal of Personality and Social Psychology* 37 (1979): 1097–1126.

Fengler, Alfred P., and Leif Jensen. "Perceived and Objective Conditions as Predictors of the Life Satisfaction of Urban and Non-Urban Elderly." *Journal of Gerontology* 36 (November 1981): 750–52.

Ferstl, Kenneth. "Public Librarians and Service to the Aging: A Study of Attitudes." Ph.D. diss., Indiana University, 1977.

Fisch, L. "Special Senses: The Aging Auditory System." In *Textbook of Geriatric Medicine and Gerontology*, 276–90. Ed. by J. C. Brocklehurst. New York: Churchill Livingstone, 1978.

Fischer, J., et al. "Life-Cycle Career Patterns: A Typological Approach to Female Status Attainment." *Technical Bulletin* 8 (March 1979) (University of Alabama: Center for the Study of Aging).

Foner, Anne, and Karen Schwab. *Aging and Retirement*. Monterey, Calif.: Brooks/Cole, 1981.

Fowles, Donald G., comp. *A Profile of Older Americans: 1991*. Brochure prepared by the Program Resources Department, American Association of Retired Persons and the Administration on Aging, U.S. Department of Health and Human Resources. Washington, D.C.: U.S. Government Printing Office, 1991.

Gallego, D. "The Mexican American Elderly: Familial and Friendship Support System . . . Fact or Fiction?" Paper read at the annual meeting of the Gerontological Society of America, San Diego, 1980.

Garcia, Alejandro. "Social Policy and Elderly Hispanic." In *Hispanic Elderly in Transition: Theory, Research, Policy, and Practice*. Ed. by Steven R. Applewhite. New York: Greenwood Press, 1988.

Gelfand, Donald E. *The Aging Network: Programs and Services*. 2d ed. New York: Springer, 1984.

———. *The Aging Network: Programs and Services*. 3d ed. New York: Springer, 1988.

Gelfand, Donald E., and Charles M. Barresi, eds. *Ethnic Dimensions of Aging*. New York: Springer, 1987.

George, Linda K. *Role Transitions in Later Life*. Monterey, Calif.: Brooks/Cole, 1980.

Gerace, Cheryl Stewart, and Linda S. Noelker. "Clinical Social Work Practice with Black Elderly and Their Family Caregivers." In *Black Aged: Understanding Diversity and Service Needs*, 236–58. Ed. by Zev Harel, Edward A. McKinney, and Michael Williams. Newbury Park, Calif.: Sage, 1990.

Gibb, Jack R. *Trust: A New View of Personal and Organizational Development*. Los Angeles: The Guild of Tutors Press, 1978.

Gibson, Rose C. "Defining Retirement for Black Americans." In *Ethnic Dimensions of Aging*, 224–38. Ed. by Donald E. Gelfand and Charles M. Barresi. New York: Springer, 1987.

Glendenning, Frank, ed. *Educational Gerontology, International Perspectives*. New York: St. Martin's Press, 1985.

Glick, Ira O., and Sidney J. Levy. *Living with Television*. Chicago: Aldine, 1962.

Goffman, Erving. *Behavior in Public Places*. New York: Free Press, 1963.

Goode, William J. "A Theory of Role Strain." *American Sociological Review* 25 (August 1960): 483–96.

Gove, Walter, et al. "The Family Life Cycle: Internal Dynamics and Social Consequences." *Sociology and Social Research* 57 (January 1973): 182–95.

Grabowski, Stanley, and W. Dean Mason, eds. *Learning for Aging*. Washington, D.C.: Adult Education Association of the U.S.A., 1974.

Gray, Robert M., and David O. Moberg. *The Church and the Other Person.* Grand Rapids, Mich.: Eerdmans, 1977.

Greene, Roberta R. *Social Work with the Aged and Their Families.* New York: Aldine de Gruyter, 1986.

"Guidelines for Library Service to Older Adults." Prepared by the Library Services to an Aging Population Committee, Reference and Adult Services Division, American Library Association. Adopted by the Reference and Adult Services Division Board of Directors, January 1987. *RQ* 26 (Summer 1987): 444–47.

Gumpert, Gary, and Robert Cathecart, eds. *Intermedia: Interpersonal Communication in a Media World.* 3d ed. New York: Oxford University Press, 1986.

Gunderson, E. K. Eric, and Richard H. Rahe, eds. *Life Stress and Illness.* Springfield, Ill.: C. C. Thomas, 1974.

Hales, Celia. *How Should the Information Needs of the Aging Be Met?* Minneapolis: University of Minnesota Libraries, ERIC Document Reproduction Service No. 294 582, 1987.

______. "How Should the Information Needs of the Aging Be Met? A Delphi Response." *The Gerontologist* 25 (April 1985): 172–76.

______. "Planning for the Information Needs of the Aging: A Delphi Study." Ph.D. diss., Florida State University, 1982.

Hales-Mabry, Celia. "Basic Ways to Communicate with Elders." In *Unequal Access to Information Resources: Problems and Needs of the World's Information Poor: Proceedings of the Congress for Librarians, February 17, 1986, Including Related Invited Papers and a Classified Bibliography, St. John's University, Jamaica, New York,* 113–17. Edited by Jovian Lang. Ann Arbor, Mich.: Pierian Press, 1988.

______. "The Reactors: Celia Hales-Mabry." In *Information and Aging: Proceedings of the Twenty-fifth Annual Symposium of the Graduate Alumni and Faculty of the Rutgers School of Communication, Information, and Library Studies, 9 April 1987,* 55–57. Ed. by Betty J. Turock. Jefferson, N.C.: McFarland, 1988.

______. "Serving the Older Adult." In *The Reference Library User,* 69–76. Ed. by Bill Katz. New York: Haworth Press, 1990.

Hampe, Gary D., and Audie L. Blevins, Jr. "Primary Group Interaction and Residents in a Retirement Hotel." *International Journal of Aging and Human Development* 6 (1975): 309–20.

Harbert, Anita S., and Leon H. Ginsberg. *Human Services for Older Adults.* Belmont, Calif.: Wadsworth, 1979.

______. *Human Services for Older Adults: Concepts and Skills.* Columbia, S.C.: University of South Carolina Press, 1990.

Harel, Zev, Phyllis Ehrlich, and Richard Hubbard. *The Vulnerable Aged: People, Services, and Policies.* New York: Springer, 1990.

Harel, Zev, et al., eds. *Black Aged: Understanding Diversity and Service Needs*. Newbury Park, Calif.: Sage, 1990.

Harris, Adrienne E. "Social Dialectics and Language: Mother and Child Construct the Discourse." *Human Development* 18 (1975): 80–96.

Harris, Louis, et al. *Aging in the Eighties: America in Transition*. Washington, D.C.: National Council on the Aging, 1981.

______. *The Myth and Reality of Aging in America*. Washington, D.C.: National Council on the Aging, 1975.

Havighurst, R. J., and Augusta De Vries. "Life-Styles and Free Time Activities of Retired Men." *Human Development* 12 (1969): 34–54.

Heeks, Peggy, and Elaine Kempson, eds. *Meeting the Needs of Elderly People—The Public Library's Role; Proceedings of a British Library Seminar Held on November 30th 1984*. Winchester, England: Public Libraries Research Group, 1985.

Hendricks, Jon. *Aging in Mass Society: Myths and Realities*. Cambridge, Mass.: Winthrop, 1981.

Hendrickson, Michael C., ed. "The Role of the Church in Aging: Implications for Policy and Action." *Journal of Religion and Aging* 2 (1985–86): 5–16.

Hessel, Dieter, ed. *Maggie Kuhn on Aging: A Dialogue Edited by Dieter Hessel*. Philadelphia: Westminster Press, 1977.

Hill, Reuben. "Decision Making and the Family Life Cycle." In *Social Structures and the Family*, 113–39. Ed. by Ethel Shanas and Gordon F. Streib. Englewood Cliffs, N.J.: Prentice-Hall, 1965.

Huttman, Elizabeth D. *Social Services for the Elderly*. New York: Free Press, 1985.

Jackson, Jacqueline Johnson. *Minorities and Aging*. Belmont, Calif.: Wadsworth, 1980.

Jackson, James S., et al., eds. *The Black American Elderly: Research on Physical and Psychosocial Health*. New York: Springer, 1988.

Jackson, James S., and Rose C. Gibson. "Work and Retirement among the Black Elderly." In *Current Perspectives on Aging and the Life Cycle*, vol. 1, 193–222. Ed by Zena Blau. Greenwich, Conn.: JAI Press, 1985.

John, Robert. *American Indian Aging*. Washington, D.C.: Association for Gerontology in Higher Education, 1988.

Johnson, Harold R., Rose C. Gibson, and Irene Luckey. "Health and Social Characteristics: Implications for Services." In *Black Aged: Understanding Diversity and Service Needs*, 69–81. Ed. by Zev Harel, Edward A. McKinney, and Michael Williams. Newbury Park, Calif.: Sage, 1990.

Johnstone, John Wallace Claire, and Ramon J. Rivera. *Volunteers for Learning: A Study of the Educational Pursuits of American Adults*. Chicago: Aldine, 1965.

Jones, Reginald L. *Black Adult Development and Aging*. Berkeley, Calif.: Cobb & Henry, 1989.

Jung, C. G. "Psychotherapie und Seelsorge," in *Die Gesammelten Werke von C. G. Jung*. Zurich: Rascher, 1958–70.

Kahana, Eva, Boaz Kahana, and Jennifer Kinney. "Coping among Vulnerable Elders." In *The Vulnerable Aged: People, Services, and Policies*, 64–85. Ed. by Zev Harel, Phyllis Ehrlich, and Richard Hubbard. New York: Springer, 1990.

Kart, Cary Steven. *The Realities of Aging: An Introduction to Gerontology*. 2d ed. Boston: Allyn & Bacon, 1985.

Kenney, Richard A. *Physiology of Aging: A Synopsis*. Chicago: Year Book Medical Publishers, 1982.

Keyfitz, Nathan, and Wilhelm Flieger. *World Population Growth and Aging: Demographic Trends in the Late Twentieth Century*. Chicago: University of Chicago Press, 1990.

Klapper, Joseph T. *The Effects of Mass Communication*. Glencoe, Ill.: Free Press, 1960.

Koenig, Harold George, Mona Smiley, and Jo Ann Ploch Gonzales. *Religion, Health, and Aging: A Review and Theoretical Integration*. New York: Greenwood Press, 1988.

Kovar, M. G. "Aging in the Eighties: Preliminary Data from the Supplement on Aging to the National Health Interview Survey, United States, January–June, 1984." In *Advanced Data from Vital and Health Statistics of the National Center for Health Statistics* (No. 115, DHHS Publication No. PHS 86–1250). Hyattsville, Md.: U.S. Public Health Service, 1986.

Krauss, I. "Individual Differences in Reactions to Retirement." Paper read at the annual meeting of the Gerontological Society of America and the Canadian Association on Gerontology, Toronto, November 1981.

Kunkel, S. R., and R. A. Applebaum. "The Future of Long-Term Care: Projections and Challenges." Paper read at the annual meeting of the Gerontological Society of America, San Francisco, November 1988.

Lammers, William W., and David Klingman. *State Policies and the Aging: Sources, Trends, and Options*. Lexington, Mass.: Lexington Books, 1984.

Landsberger, Betty H. *Long-Term Care for the Elderly: A Comparative View of Layers of Care*. New York: St. Martin's Press, 1985.

Lang, Gerrit, et al. *Personal Conversations: Roles and Skills for Counsellors*. London: Routledge, 1990.

Langer, Ellen J., et al. "Environmental Determinants of Memory Improvement in Late Adulthood." *Journal of Personality and Social Psychology* 37 (November 1979): 2003–2013.

Laslett, Peter. *The World We Have Lost*. 2d ed. London: Methuen, 1971.

Lasswell, Harold D. "The Structure and Function of Communication in Society." In *The Communication of Ideas*, 37–52. Ed. by Lyman Bryson. New York: Harper, 1946.

Lawton, M. Powell. "The Impact of the Environment on Aging and Behavior." In *Handbook of the Psychology of Aging*, 276–301. Ed. by James E. Birren and K. Warner Schaie. New York: Van Nostrand, 1977.

Leanse, Joyce, and Sara B. Wagner. *Senior Centers: A Report of Senior Group Programs in America*. Washington, D.C.: National Council on the Aging, 1975.

Lee, Jik-Joen. "Asian American Elderly: A Neglected Minority Group." In *Ethnicity and Gerontological Social Work*, 103–16. Ed. by Rose Dobrof. New York: Haworth Press, 1987.

Lehman, Harvey C. "The Age Decrement in Outstanding Scientific Creativity." *American Psychologist* 15 (February 1960): 128–34.

Lemon, Bruce W., Vern L. Bengston, and James A. Peterson. "An Exploration of the Activity Theory of Aging: Activity Types and Life Satisfaction among the Movers in a Retirement Community." *Journal of Gerontology* 27 (October 1972): 511–23.

Lesnoff-Caravaglie, Gari, ed. *Values, Ethnics, and Aging*. New York: Human Sciences Press, 1985.

Levenson, Alvin J., and Dianna M. Porter, eds. *An Introduction to Gerontology and Geriatrics: A Multi-Disciplinary Approach*. Springfield, Ill.: C. C. Thomas, 1984.

Lewis, Sandra Cutler. *Providing for the Older Adult: A Gerontological Handbook*. Thorofare, N.J.: Slack, 1983.

Lopata, Helena Znaniecka. *Widowhood in an American City*. Cambridge, Mass.: Schenkman, 1973.

______. *Women as Widows: Support Systems*. New York: Elsevier/North Holland, 1979.

Louis Harris and Associates, Inc. *Aging in the Eighties: America in Transition: A Survey*. Washington, D.C.: National Council on the Aging, 1981.

______. *The Myth and Reality of Aging in America*. Washington, D.C.: National Council on the Aging, 1975.

Lowenthal, Marjorie Fiske, and Betsy Robinson. "Social Networks and Isolation." In *Handbook of Aging and the Social Sciences*. Ed. by Robert H. Binstock and Ethel Shanas. New York: Van Nostrand, 1976.

Lowenthal, Marjorie Fiske, Betsy Robinson, and Clayton Haven. "Interaction and Adaptation: Intimacy as a Critical Variable." *American Sociological Review* 33 (February 1968): 20–30.

Lowy, Louis. *Why Education in the Later Years?* Lexington, Mass.: Lexington Books, 1986.

Lubben, James E., and Rosina M. Becerra. "Social Support among Black, Mexican, and Chinese Elderly." In *Ethnic Dimensions of Aging*, 130–44. Ed. by Donald E. Gelfand and Charles M. Barresi. New York: Springer, 1987.

Maas, Henry S., and Joseph A. Kuypers. *From Thirty to Seventy*. 1st ed. San Francisco: Jossey-Bass, 1974.

McClusky, Howard Y. "Education for Aging: The Scope of the Field and Perspectives for the Future." In *Learning for Aging*, 324–55. Ed. by Stanley M. Grabowski and W. Dean Mason. Washington, D.C.: Adult Education Association, 1974.

MacCrae, Robert R. "Age Differences in the Use of Coping Mechanisms." *Journal of Gerontology* 37 (July 1982): 454–60.

McGarry, K. J. *Communication Knowledge and the Librarian*. London: C. Bingley, 1975; Hamden, Conn.: Linnet Books, 1975.

MacLean, Doug, and Sue Gould. *The Helping Process: An Introduction*. London: Croom Helm, 1988.

MacLean, Michael J., and Rita Bonar. "Cooperative Practice to Overcome Socially Constructed Hardship for Ethnic Elderly People." In *Ethnic Dimensions of Aging*, 211–35. Ed. by Donald E. Gelfand and Charles M. Barresi. New York: Springer, 1987.

McPherson, Barry D. *Aging as a Social Process: An Introduction to Individual and Population Aging*. Toronto: Butterworths, 1983.

McPherson, J. Miller, and Lynn Smith-Lovin. "Women and Weak Ties: Differences by Sex in the Size of Voluntary Associations." *American Journal of Sociology* 87 (January 1982): 883–904.

McQuail, Denis. *Mass Communication Theory: An Introduction*. 2d ed. London: Sage, 1987.

Mark Battle Associates. *Evaluation and Referral Services for the Elderly*. Washington, D.C.: Dept. of Health, Education, and Welfare, Office of Human Development, Administration on Aging, 1977.

Markides, Kyriakos S., and Charles H. Mindel. *Aging and Ethnicity*. Newbury Park, Calif.: Sage, 1987.

Matthews, A., and K. Brown. "Retirement and Change in Social Interaction: Objective and Subjective Assessments." Paper read at the annual meeting of the Gerontological Society of America and the Canadian Association on Gerontology, Toronto, November 1981.

Medley, Morris L. "Marital Adjustment in the Post-Retirement Years." *The Family Coordinator* 26 (January 1977): 5–11.

Meyersohn, Rolf. "A Critical Examination of Commercial Entertainment." In *Aging and Leisure*, 243–72. New York: Oxford University Press, 1961.

Mindel, Charles H., and Roosevelt Wright. "The Use of Social Services by Black and White Elderly: The Role of Social Support Systems." *Journal of Gerontological Social Work* 4 (Spring/Summer 1982): 107–26.

Mindel, Charles H., et al. "Informal and Formal Social and Health Service Use by Black and White Elderly: A Comparative Cost Approach." *Gerontologist* 26 (June 1986): 279–85.

Mitchell, Garry. "Some Aspects of Telephone Socialization." In *Studies in Mass Communication and Technology*, 249–52. Ed. by Sari Thomas. Norwood, N.J.: ABLEX, 1984.

Moberg, David O. "Christian Beliefs and Personal Adjustment in Old Age." *Journal of the American Scientific Affiliation* 10 (March 1958): 8–12.

Moeller, Leslie G. "The Big Four Mass Media: Actualities and Expectations." In *Beyond Media: New Approaches to Mass Communication*, 14–51. Ed. by Richard W. Budd and Brent D. Ruben. Rochelle Park, N.J.: Hayden, 1979.

Monk, Abraham. *Handbook of Gerontological Services*. New York: Columbia University Press, 1990.

Moss, Miriam S., and M. Powell Lawton. "Time Budgets of Oldest People: A Window on Four Lifestyles." *Journal of Gerontology* 37 (January, 1982): 115–23.

Murdock, Bennet. "Recent Developments in Short-Term Memory." *Quarterly Journal of Experimental Psychology* 18 (August 1966): 206–11.

National Center for Health Statistics. *Vital and Health Statistics: Proceedings of the 1988 International Symposium on Data on Aging*. Hyattsville, Md.: U.S. Department of Health and Human Services, 1991.

National Council on Aging. *Fact Book on Aging*. Washington, D.C.: National Council on Aging, 1978.

Neugarten, Bernice Levin. *Middle Age and Aging: A Reader in Social Psychology*. Chicago: University of Chicago Press, 1968.

Neugarten, Bernice Levin, and Karol K. Weinstein. "The Changing American Grandparent." *Journal of Marriage and the Family* 26 (May 1964): 199–204.

Neugarten, Bernice Levin, and Sheldon S. Tobin. "Personality and Patterns of Aging." In *Middle Age and Aging*, 173–77. Ed. by Bernice Neugarten. Chicago: University of Chicago Press, 1968.

Nussbaum, Jon F., Teresa Thompson, and James D. Robinson. *Communication and Aging*. New York: Harper, 1989.

Organisation for Economic Co-Operation and Development (OECD). *Ageing Populations: The Social Policy Implications*. Paris: OECD, 1988.

Orr, Douglass Winnett, and Nancy Orr Addams. *Life Cycle Counseling: Guidelines for Helping People*. Springfield, Ill.: Charles C. Thomas, 1987.

Osgood, Nancy J., and Ann H. L. Sontz, eds. *The Science and Practice of Gerontology: A Multidisciplinary Guide*. New York: Greenwood Press, 1989.

Palmore, Erdman B. "The Effects of Aging on Activities and Attitudes." *Gerontologist* 8 (Winter 1968): 259–63.

Panek, Paul E., et al. "A Review of Age Changes in Perceptual Information Processing Ability with Regard to Driving." *Experimental Aging Research* 3 (November, 1977): 387–449.

Parks, Arnold G. *Black Elderly in Rural America: A Comprehensive Study.* Bristol, Ind.: Wyndham Hall Press, 1988.

Pember, Don R. *Mass Media in America.* 5th ed. Chicago: Science Research Associates, 1987.

Pepper, Nathan Hale. *Fundamentals of Care of the Aging, Disabled, and Handicapped: In the Nursing Home.* Springfield, Ill.: C. C. Thomas, 1982.

Peterson, David A., James E. Thornton, and James E. Birren, eds. *Education and Aging.* Englewood Cliffs, N.J.: Prentice-Hall, 1986.

Peterson, Richard E. *Lifelong Learning in America.* 1st ed. San Francisco: Jossey-Bass, 1979.

Poon, Leonard W., ed. *Aging in the 1980s: Psychological Issues.* Washington, D.C.: American Psychological Association, 1980.

Poon, Leonard W., David C. Rubin, and Barbara A. Wilson. *Everyday Cognition in Adulthood and Late Life.* Cambridge, England: Cambridge University Press, 1989.

Reichard, Suzanne Kate. *Aging and Personality.* New York: Wiley, 1962.

Rice, Michael. *Toward Harnessing New Electronic Technologies to Meet the Needs of Elderly People: Report of an Aspen Institute Planning Meeting, Wye Woods Conference Center, Queenstown, Md., March 24–25, 1987.* New York: Aspen Institute for Humanistic Studies, 1987.

Robinson, Charles. "Conflicting Roles of the Public Library." In *Issues for the New Decade: Today's Challenge, Tomorrow's Opportunity,* 81–99. Ed. by Alphonse F. Trezza. Boston: G. K. Hall, 1991.

Rogers, Dorothy. *The Adult Years: An Introduction to Aging.* 2d ed. Englewood Cliffs, N.J.: Prentice-Hall, 1982.

Rollins, Boyd C., and Kenneth L. Cannon. "Marital Satisfaction over the Family Life Cycle: A Reevaluation." *Journal of Marriage and the Family* 29 (May 1974): 271–83.

Rosenmayr, Leopold, and Eva Kockeis. "Propositions for a Sociological Theory of Aging and the Family." *International Social Science Journal* 15 (1963): 410–26.

Rosow, Irving. "Housing and Local Ties of the Aged." In *Middle Age and Aging,* 382–89. Ed. by Bernice L. Neugarten. Chicago: University of Chicago Press, 1968.

______. *Social Integration of the Aged.* New York: Free Press, 1967.

Rubin, Rhea Joyce, and Gail McGovern. *Working with Older Adults: A Handbook for Libraries.* 3d ed. Sacramento: California State Library Foundation, 1990.

Rybash, John M., William J. Hoyer, and Paul A. Roodin. *Adult Cognition and Aging: Developmental Changes in Processing, Knowing and Thinking*. New York: Pergamon Press, 1986.

Santrock, John W. *Adult Development and Aging*. Dubuque, Iowa: W. C. Brown, 1985.

Sarason, Seymour Bernard. *Caring and Compassion in Clinical Practice*. lst ed. San Francisco, Calif.: Jossey-Bass, 1985.

Sauer, William J., and Raymond T. Coward, eds. *Social Support Networks and the Care of the Elderly*. New York: Springer, 1985.

Saxon, Sue V. *Physical Change and Aging: A Guide for the Helping Professions*. 2d ed. New York: Tiresias Press, 1987.

Schaie, K. Warner. "Age Changes in Adult Intelligence." In *Aging: Scientific Perspectives and Social Issues*, 111–24. Ed. by Diana Stenen Woodruff and James E. Birren. New York: Van Nostrand, 1975.

Schaie, K. Warner, ed. *Longitudinal Studies of Adult Psychological Development*. New York: Guilford Press, 1983.

Schaie, K. Warner, and Carmi Schooler, eds. *Social Structure and Aging: Psychological Processes*. Hillsdale, N.J.: L. Erlbaum Associates, 1989.

Schmitz-Scherzer, Reinhard. "Ageing and Leisure." *Society and Leisure* 2 (1979): 377–93.

Schramm, Wilbur Lang, and Donald F. Roberts, eds. *The Process and Effects of Mass Communication*. Urbana: University of Illinois Press, 1971.

Schramm, Wilbur Lang, and William E. Porter. *Men, Women, Messages, and Media*. 2d ed. New York: Harper, 1982.

Schwab, Teresa, ed. *Caring for an Aging World: International Models for Long-Term Care, Financing, and Delivery*. New York: McGraw-Hill Information Services, 1989.

Serow, William J., David F. Sly, and J. Michael Wrigley. *Population Aging in the United States*. New York: Greenwood Press, 1990.

Shanas, Ethel. "Family Help Patterns and Social Class in Three Countries." *Journal of Marriage and the Family* 29 (May 1967): 257–66.

Shanas, Ethel, and Gordon F. Streib. *Social Structure and the Family: Generational Relations and Social Structure*. Englewood Cliffs, N.J.: Prentice-Hall, 1965.

Shanas, Ethel, and Marvin B. Sussman, eds. *Family, Bureaucracy, and the Elderly*. Durham, N.C.: Duke University Press, 1977.

Shaw, Marion W., ed. *The Challenge of Ageing: A Multidisciplinary Approach to Extended Care*. Melbourne: Churchill Livingstone, 1984.

Silverstone, Barbara, and Ann Burack-Weiss. *Social Work Practice with the Frail Elderly and Their Families: The Auxiliary Function Model*. Springfield, Ill.: C. C. Thomas, 1983.

Simons, Ronald L., and Gale E. West. "Life Changes, Coping Resources and Health among the Elderly." *International Journal of Aging and Human Development* 20 (1985): 173–89.

Snow, Robert P. *Creating Media Culture*. Beverly Hills, Calif.: Sage, 1983.

Sorensen, Gloria, ed. *Older Persons and Service Providers: An Instructor's Training Guide*. New York: Human Sciences Press, 1981.

Sorensen, Gloria, and Herbert Shore. "Sensory Deprivation." In *Older Persons and Service Providers: An Instructor's Training Guide*, 46–76. Ed. by Gloria Sorensen. New York: Human Sciences Press, 1981.

Sotomayor, Marta, and Herman Curiel, eds. *Hispanic Elderly: A Cultural Signature*. Edinburg, Tex.: Pan American University Press, 1988.

Sotomayor, Marta, Herman Curiel, and Steven R. Applewhite. "The Hispanic Elderly and the Extended Multigenerational Family." In *Hispanic Elderly in Transition: Theory, Research, Policy, and Practice*, 121–34. Ed. by Steven R. Applewhite. New York: Greenwood Press, 1988.

Spirfuso, Waneen, and Priscilla Gilliam MacRae. "Motor Performance and Aging." In *Handbook of the Psychology of Aging*, 184–200. 2d ed. Ed. by James E. Birren and K. Warner Schaie. San Diego: Academic Press, 1990.

Sprott, Richard L., ed. *Age, Learning Ability, and Intelligence*. New York: Van Nostrand, 1980.

Staines, Gordon. "Spillover versus Compensation: A Review of the Literature on the Relationship between Work and Nonwork." *Human Relations* 33 (February 1980): 111–29.

Stanford, E. Percil. "Diverse Black Aged." In *Black Age: Understanding Diversity and Service Needs*, 33–49. Ed. by Zev Harel, Edward McKinney, and Michael Williams. Newbury Park, Calif.: Sage, 1990.

Stinnett, Nick, Linda Mittelstet Cart, and James E. Montgomery. "Older Persons' Perceptions of Their Marriages." *Journal of Marriage and the Family* 34 (November 1972): 665–70.

Streib, Gordon F. "Intergenerational Relations: Perspectives of the Two Generations on the Older Parent." *Journal of Marriage and the Family* 27 (November 1965): 469–76.

———. "Social Stratification and Aging." In *Handbook of Aging and the Social Sciences*, 160–88. Ed. by Robert H. Binstock and Ethel Shanas. New York: Van Nostrand, 1976.

Stub, Holger Richard. *The Social Consequences of Long Life*. Springfield, Ill.: C. C. Thomas, 1982.

Sussman, Marvin B. "The Family Life of Old People." In *Handbook of Aging and the Social Sciences*, 218–43. Ed. by Robert H. Binstock and Ethel Shanas. New York: Van Nostrand, 1976.

Sussman, Marvin B., and Lee Burchinal. "Kin Family Network: Unheralded Structure in Current Conceptualizations of Family Functioning." *Marriage and Family Living* 24 (August 1962): 231–40.

Taeuber, Cynthia. "Sixty-Five Plus in the U.S.A." Unpublished paper. Washington, D.C.: Bureau of the Census, Population Division, 1992?

Taeuber, Cynthia, and Arnold A. Goldstein. "The 1990 Census and the Older Population: Data for Researchers, Planners, and Practitioners." Unpublished paper. Washington, D.C.: Bureau of the Census, Population Division, 1992?

Tamir, Lois M. *Communication and the Aging Process: Interaction throughout the Life Cycle*. New York: Pergamon Press, 1979.

______. "The Older Person's Communication Needs: The Perspective of Developmental Psychology." In *Communications Technology and the Elderly: Issues and Forecasts*, 28–31. Ed. by Ruth E. Dunkle, Marie R. Haugh, and Marvin Rosenberg. New York: Springer, 1984.

Taylor, Robert Joseph, and Linda M. Chatters. "Family, Friend, and Church Support Networks of Black Americans." In *Black Adult Development and Aging*, 245–72. Ed. by Reginald L. Jones. Berkeley, Calif.: Cobb & Henry, 1989.

Thomas, Sari. *Studies in Mass Communication and Technology: Selected Proceedings from the Fourth International Conference on Culture and Communication, Temple University, 1981*. Norwood, N.J.: ABLEX, 1984.

Tobin, Sheldon S., James W. Ellor, and Susan M. Anderson-Ray. *Enabling the Elderly: Religious Institutions within the Community Service System*. Albany: State University of New York Press, 1986.

Tobin, Sheldon S., et al. *Last Home for the Aged*. San Francisco: Jossey-Bass, 1976.

Torres-Gil, Fernando. "Aging in an Ethnic Society: Policy Issues for Aging among Minority Groups." In *Ethnic Dimensions of Aging*, 239–57. Ed. by Donald E. Gelfand and Charles M. Barresi. New York: Springer, 1987.

Torrey, Barbara Boyle, Kevin Kinselia, and Cynthia M. Taeuber. *An Aging World*. International Population Reports Series P-95, No. 78. Washington, D.C.: U.S. Government Printing Office, 1987.

Townsend, Aloen, and Zev Harel. "Health Vulnerability and Service Need among the Aged." In *The Vulnerable Aged: People, Services, and Policies*, 32–52. Ed. by Zev Harel, Phyllis Ehrlich, and Richard Hubbard. New York: Springer, 1990.

Treat, Nancy J., and Hayne W. Reese. "Age, Pacing, and Imagery in Paired-Associate Learning." *Developmental Psychology* 12 (March 1976): 119–24.

Troll, Lillian E. "The Family in Later Life: A Decade Review." *Journal of Marriage and the Family* 33 (May 1971): 263–90.

Troll, Lillian E., and Jean Smith. "Attachment through the Life Span: Some Questions about Dyadic Bonds among Adults." *Human Development* 19 (1976): 156–70.

Truax, Charles B., and Robert R. Carkhuff. *Toward Effective Counseling and Psychotherapy: Training and Practice.* Chicago: Aldine, 1967.

Turner, Barbara F., Sheldon S. Tobin, and Morton A. Lieberman. "Personality Traits as Predictors of Institutional Adaptation among the Aged." *Journal of Gerontology* 27 (January 1972): 61–68.

Turock, Betty J. *Serving the Older Adult: A Guide to Library Programs and Information Sources.* New York: Bowker, 1982.

Van Tassel, David, and Peter N. Stearns, eds. *Old Age in a Bureaucratic Society: The Elderly, the Experts, and the State in American History.* Westport, Conn.: Greenwood Press, 1986.

Vincente, Leticia, James A. Wiley, and R. Allen Carrington. "The Risk of Institutionalization before Death." *Gerontologist* 19 (August 1979): 361–67.

Walsh, David A. "Age Differences in Learning and Memory." In *Aging: Scientific Perspectives and Social Issues*, 125–51. Ed. by Diana S. Woodruff and James E. Birren. New York: Van Nostrand, 1975.

Ward, Russell A. *The Aging Experience: An Introduction to Social Gerontology.* 2d ed. New York: Harper, 1984.

Watson, Wilbur H. "Family Care, Economics, and Health." In *Black Aged: Understanding Diversity and Service Needs*, 50–68. Ed. by Zev Harel, Edward A. McKinney, and Michael Williams. Newbury Park, Calif.: Sage, 1990.

Wehr, Gerhard. *Jung: A Biography.* Trans. David M. Weeks. Boston: Shambhala, 1987.

Whitbourne, Susan Krauss. *The Aging Body: Physiological Changes and Psychological Consequences.* New York: Springer-Verlag, 1985.

Wilson, John. "Sociology of Leisure." *Annual Review of Sociology* 6 (1980): 21–40.

Wolinsky, Fredric D., Rodney M. Coe, and Ray R. Mosely. "The Use of Health Services by Elderly Americans: Implications from a Regression-Based Cohort Analysis." In *Health in Aging: Sociological Issues*, 106–32. Ed. by Russell A. Ward and Sheldon S. Tobin. New York: Springer, 1987.

Woodruff, Diana Stenen, and James E. Birren, eds. *Aging: Scientific Perspectives and Social Issues.* New York: Van Nostrand, 1975.

______. *Aging: Scientific Perspectives and Social Issues.* Monterey, Calif.: Brooks/Cole, 1983.

Zopf, Paul E. *American's Older Population.* Houston: Cap and Gown Press, 1986.

# NAME INDEX

# SUBJECT INDEX

Celia Hales-Mabry has ten years' service as a reference librarian in university settings, the most recent seven at the University of Minnesota. She received her education from Florida State University (Ph.D., Library Science), East Carolina State University (M.L.S.), and Duke University (M.A., B.A. in English). She has researched and published in the area of information needs of older adults since 1979. Hales-Mabry lives in St. Paul with her husband, Paul, a psychologist on the faculty of the University of St. Thomas.